What Will They Say?

What Will They Say?

CONFRONT CULTURAL TABOOS AND DISCOVER YOUR INNER POWER

DENISE SOLER COX

PRIMERO
SUEÑO PRESS

ATRIA

NEW YORK AMSTERDAM/ANTWERP LONDON
TORONTO SYDNEY/MELBOURNE NEW DELHI

PRIMERO
SUEÑO PRESS

ATRIA
An Imprint of Simon & Schuster, LLC
1230 Avenue of the Americas
New York, NY 10020

Names and identifying details have been changed.

First Primero Sueño Press/Atria Books hardcover edition August 2026

PRIMERO SUEÑO PRESS / ATRIA BOOKS and colophon are registered trademarks of Simon & Schuster, LLC

Interior design by Kyoko Watanabe

Manufactured in the United States of America

1 3 5 7 9 10 8 6 4 2

The Library of Congress Cataloging-in-Publication Data has been applied for.

ISBN 978-1-6680-8296-6
ISBN 978-1-6680-8298-0 (ebook)

For Georgie and Phoebe, my greatest teachers and the most exquisite humans I know. May you always trust: the girl who dreams is never lost, she's just waiting for you to remember her.

and i said to my body. softly. "i want to be your friend."
it took a long breath. and replied "i have been waiting
my whole life for this."

—NAYYIRAH WAHEED

CONTENTS

CONTENTS

INTRODUCTION

Why Do Latinas Need This Book?

The narrative about Latina women in America is outdated and incomplete. While popular culture focuses on the immigrant experience, the reality is that 68 percent of Latinas are born in the United States. We're not newcomers trying to assimilate—we're navigating something far more complex.

We're caught between two worlds with two different sets of rules, and it's showing up in our professional lives in ways that are finally being documented. According to Lean In and McKinsey's comprehensive *Women in the Workplace 2024* report,[1] "women of color continue to deal with more demeaning interactions" at work, and this issue "is even worse for women of color" than for their white colleagues. Research focused on Latina women shows we face intercultural discrimination that directly impacts our performance—from being told to be "less emotional," "less expressive," or "less loud," to facing systemic barriers where 53 percent of Latinas report that executive presence is defined by "conforming to traditionally white male standards."[2]

This isn't just about workplace bias. It's about the internal conflict of trying to succeed in systems that weren't built for us, while staying true to cultural values that are actually strengths—but are often misunderstood or devalued.

It's time to confront these challenges head-on by unpacking the sources both external and internal and finding a new way to build community, support, and cultural pride that doesn't require us to choose between authenticity and success.

I decided to write this book because after nearly a decade of speaking to audiences and coaching ambitious Latinas, I kept seeing the same pattern: brilliant women stuck, not because they lacked talent or drive, but because they'd lost touch with who they were before the world told them how to succeed, trying to navigate success with a road map that didn't account for their reality instead of giving themselves permission to want more.

Why I Wrote This Book

For almost a decade, I've traveled the country sharing my documentary, *being eñye*, about the unique identity challenges of being first-generation in this country. I hoped that audiences would feel seen, but I was surprised by what emerged from their reactions. After every screening, lines of Latina women would wait to share their stories with me, and what started as conversations about identity became something much bigger. I began hearing the same patterns everywhere: in my coaching programs, speaking events, and countless one-on-one conversations.

Over the years, I heard variations of the same themes: women sacrificing everything to protect and serve their families—staying silent about trauma, turning down opportunities, shrinking themselves to fit cultural expectations about success, money, visibility, relationships, and what it means to be "good." Every secret they shared was attached to an unfulfilled dream, and in every case, their adherence to unspoken cultural rules was the strongest barrier to their aspirations.

We weren't just carrying personal shame. We were carrying generations of rules about what we could want, who we could be, and how much we were allowed to dream.

Inheritances

There are two forces in particular that shape us as Latinas.

The first: family secrets
The stories kept hidden, the facts buried in shame.

The second: cultural taboos
The unspoken rules about what we can want, who we can be, how much space we can take up.

As Latinas, we're brought up with contradictory beliefs that are meant to root us in shared culture but often end up holding us back. These unspoken rules show up in how we discredit our very existence:

- Don't make everything about you.
- Don't be too successful.
- Don't ask for help.

These taboos are maddening because they conflict with what success actually requires—visibility, ambition, and the willingness to seek support. We're caught between honoring our culture and pursuing our dreams, never quite sure which set of rules to follow.

Understanding these generational cycles unlocked something in me. Not just about my family's story, but about my own. I started seeing the commonalities, how I'd learned to hold back, to deflect, to make myself smaller, and how I learned that part of being "good" meant not "making waves."

But seeing a pattern and changing it are two different things. Sometimes you need a mirror not just to see yourself, but to recognize your reflection in others who carry the same things.

No Apologizing in EDA

By this point in my life, I had spent decades trying to figure out why I couldn't exhale and relax. Meditation was something for other people; I just couldn't get there in my body. Therapy helped. Seminars helped. But it wasn't until I sat in a virtual circle of women, all of them Latina like me, our lives shaped by the same kind of struggle, that I finally understood how heavy the shame I'd been carrying was.

Year after year, women shared their secrets with me after screenings. I knew I wanted to help them somehow—but I was still carrying my own shame and had no idea how to handle theirs. What I did know was how to turn ideas into reality. I'd always been entrepreneurial, and when women would share not just their secrets but also their business ideas and dreams, I felt strongly that I could help them get those projects off the ground.

I never wanted to leave them hanging after these screenings. The whole purpose of *being eñye* was to help a generation of people feel less alone, and I yearned to keep that inspiration alive and to give it real, positive consequences in the world.

That's when I created the Eñye Dream Accelerator (EDA), a coaching program designed to help ambitious Latina women launch their projects. I knew for sure I could help them with that part. What to do with the secrets? That would take me much longer to figure out.

We'd work on marketing strategies, launch timelines, and taking uncomfortable action to make their visions real. I shared how I'd moved past certain career blocks, offered new ways of looking at challenges, and created a course they could work through on their own time. The focus was on mindset and practical steps.

What it became was something else entirely.

A transformation.

Each call felt like walking into a sanctuary built by and for us. A place where nothing had to be suppressed, and nothing was off-limits to share. Where no one flinched when the tears started. Where I'd coach someone on exactly what to say to land their first client and they'd break down, not because they didn't want success, but because they'd never considered it was possible for them. When I'd give them specific verbiage for how to talk about their expertise, they'd grapple with "Who do I think I am to say that?"

These weren't women with existing businesses worried about raising prices—most had never charged for anything. They'd joined the program because they were ready to step into a bigger version of themselves, but when I gave them the actual road map—the mindset work, the specific language, the concrete steps—they hit a wall around their worthiness and capacity to step into what was possible.

It was clear they'd never had anyone they could talk to about this, to get their questions answered in this way. They could see the woman they wanted to become, they had hints she was waiting for them, but there was stuff in between that needed to be addressed before they could embrace her.

I'd already gone through the Stanford Latino Entrepreneurship Initiative, a program created in partnership with the Latino Business Action Network (LBAN) to close the overwhelming funding and mentorship gap facing Latino entrepreneurs. The leadership development gap was so significant that Stanford created an entire curriculum around it. I was fortunate to be in the fourth cohort, and I recognized these women needed that same specific mentorship—not just theory, but real-world, culturally attuned support that we're simply not taught to seek.

That's exactly what I worked to provide them.

The emotion around charging for our services was intense. We were crossing the worthiness chasm together, bumping up against negative assessments of what was "realistic" given the earning limits they'd seen their parents hit in their lifetimes. Visibility was another huge trigger. We couldn't relate to the "fail in public" bro marketing advice. So much was riding on our success; that kind of thinking didn't track. But when they saw me out there slaying the same dragons, they knew they could too.

These women were brilliant at holding space for one another. The successful Mexican journalist, the Puerto Rican HR leader in higher education, the Peruvian pastor, the Honduran medical-device sales rep, the Mexican attorney, the Salvadoran former business owner starting over after having three children, the Dominican children's book author. They showed up on every call to tell the truth about how scary it was to step outside their established professional identities, how automatic it felt to shrink when claiming entrepreneurial authority, and how much harder it was to believe in themselves than it was to believe in everyone else.

Some of these fears they voiced out loud. But what struck me most was how they apologized. Constantly.

For everything.

"Sorry, I'm crying. I don't know why I'm so upset about this." "Sorry, I'm talking too much, someone else should go now." "Sorry, I know I sound confused; I should be paying more attention."

Every apology was a taboo speaking.

Sorry for having feelings.

Sorry for taking up space.

Sorry for not being perfect.

So I made a rule:

No apologizing in EDA.

It started as a strongly worded suggestion. Then it became our ritual. Before long, they started interrupting when someone apologized, and eventually everyone stopped apologizing for existing.

It was, in a word, divine.

I didn't just offer mentorship to help them achieve their goals. I was there to challenge the cultural belief systems that made their dreams feel impossible.

They witnessed one another with a kind of reverence I can still feel. Each woman brought not just her vision, but also her *blocks* (my word for what's standing in her way), her shame, and her grief. And what happened on those calls felt supernatural.

At first, I thought impostor syndrome was our biggest collective issue. But the more I listened, the more I realized that what we were facing wasn't just self-doubt. It was something much older and deeper.

It was cultural dissonance. The persistent frustration of trying to live by one set of rules—familial, internal, unspoken—in a world that measured us by another.

Most of us weren't struggling with whether we were good enough. We were trying to navigate the liminal space between who we are, and who we were taught to be—a bona fide collective cultural wound.

And it's so damn subtle you almost miss it.

After a while, I came to understand these women weren't just my clients; they were my teachers and they reminded me, week after week, of one of my hardest-won life lessons:

We can be both powerful and unfinished.

But the biggest revelation came from a client of mine named Nancy. Nancy was one of the most reserved and most steady of the group. She never missed a session. One day she shared that she'd received another grant to help fund her work. At this point, she'd received several of these, many over $10,000 each. Her win wasn't just a win; it was a "scream into your pillow and pop the champagne" win. But when she told us, she smiled nervously and said, "I still can't believe it."

The group erupted. Cheering, clapping, affirming every ounce of her power. But she looked stunned. As if the reality were just hitting her. As if our excitement was showing her just how big this really was.

I couldn't shake that moment.

Because what I saw in Nancy is something I see in so many Latinas I coach—and . . . in myself.

We achieve things, but we're still wrestling with what those triumphs mean. And when others celebrate us, we're stunned by their excitement because it still doesn't feel real.

For years I saw this pattern but couldn't articulate it. Now I can.

Surprise is what we feel when our work has crossed the worthiness chasm but our mind is still catching up.

When someone offers to support you, and your reflex is *Really? For me?*

That's what it feels like when you're in the space between what happened and what you believe you can achieve.

Seeing the world this way is not your fault. This stems from being trained our entire lives to stay small, selfless, and resilient. When we've grown up believing that getting support is a luxury, and that asking for it feels like crossing a line, and actually receiving it must be earned ten times over.

Living by mottoes such as:

- Don't ask for too much.
- Don't be a burden.
- Don't be difficult.
- Don't make anyone uncomfortable.
- Don't embarrass us.

So, when good things happen such as success, support, and recognition, we feel off and out of alignment.

As if someone made a mistake by choosing us.

That's why I wrote this book: to help you see that these patterns aren't personal failures; they're cultural imprints that were never meant to define us and that we can choose to heal. To give you permission to question rules you never agreed to. And to show you it's possible to bridge that gap between who you've been and who you're meant to become. We'll go through ten of these common beliefs and show you exactly how to break through while still staying the same proud Latina you've always been.

Aquí vamos, amiga. This ride changed my life. I hope it does the same for yours.

With so much love and belief in you,
Denise

CHAPTER ONE

Los Trapos Sucios Se Lavan en Casa: How to Break the Spell

There are two types of Latina daughters: the ones who speak, and the ones who keep the peace.

I figured out early which one I was supposed to be. And when you choose silence, you start to see how fragile the line really is.

There's a paper-thin veil between chaos and silence, between the story that made you and the one you get to tell now. As Latinas, we're taught to survive first and heal later (if at all). We're taught to stay and say nothing, remain grateful, and above all be loyal. Even when the house is on fire, we still protect the family name.

We're told that our parents did their best under the circumstances. That other people had it worse. That we should be grateful. The thing is, the shame of growing up in a house full of secrets doesn't vanish, it just becomes the soundtrack of your life.

Often in our families, a good daughter knows better than to speak out.

Alcoholism becomes "Papi works hard and needs to relax."

Domestic violence becomes "They have a passionate marriage."

Depression becomes "She's just too sensitive."

Sexual abuse becomes . . . nothing.

We internalize this conditioning so early, we forget it has a shape. We become the peacekeepers, the secret-keepers, the ones who absorb everything so the family stays intact.

But all that secrecy has a cost.

This book, and this chapter, is about breaking that cycle. Not to shame the people who raised us, but to honor the truth that will save us. Because you can't guard their feelings and liberate yourself at the same time.

In Latino families, there's an unwritten rule: Los trapos sucios se lavan en casa. Family business is family business, period. We don't talk about what happens, and we definitely don't share it with outsiders.

I've learned that the very thing that taught us to keep secrets also taught us to betray our own dreams. When you spend your life calculating the cost of speaking your truth, you also learn to calculate the cost of pursuing what you want. And eventually, you stop hoping for both.

The question isn't whether you have secrets worth sharing or a life worth pursuing. The question is, What's it costing you to keep them buried?

Speaking of honesty, can I share something? For most of my life, I thought courage meant not being scared. I waited way too long for that magical moment when I wouldn't feel afraid anymore.

Heads-up: That time never comes. What I now understand is how to make space for my fear—right beside me—while I do scary things anyway. The fear is like a child riding shotgun in a speeding car. Petrified, but still trusting me to drive.

I let her be afraid, and I go ahead and do the thing for both of us.

Hell, I'm terrified of writing this book, and we're only on chapter one. But I'm doing it scared.

Turns out, the story I was most afraid to tell is the one that's setting me free.

That's how, at the age of twenty-two, I ended up at a Holiday Inn ballroom in Miami Beach, sitting in a three-day personal development seminar when a memory from when I was nine suddenly, and for the very first time, flooded into my consciousness.

This was the early nineties, before South Beach's legendary resurgence. The long stretch of sand was in its final decline—crowds of white-haired retirees spent their days sitting on folding aluminum chairs playing dominoes on concrete patios of faded art deco hotels whose glamorous heyday had long passed. In just a few years, these crumbling hotels would be torn down and rebuilt as luxury destinations. The dying beach would become more vibrant than it had ever been.

I was there for my own transformation.

My friend and coworker Zach had turned me onto this experience. When he floated into the newspaper ad department where we worked, looking like a completely different man with an unshakable aura of peace, I wanted to know how.

It took $875 and one Friday off from my job to begin my own unraveling.

I sat in the audience on day one desperate for a breakthrough. But as soon as that memory came flooding in, my father's hands and the way I'd disappear inside my body, I gasped for air and shoved it back down underneath the salty water of my memory and prayed for it to drown.

Fuck breakthroughs.

This was sacred family territory and absolutely off-limits. There was no sharing with my partner seated next to me. No processing. I was there for healing, but not at the cost of betraying my family.

For many of us, family loyalty isn't just a value, it's how the multitudes of generations that came before us stayed safe. In times when saying the wrong thing to the wrong person could cost you everything, when governments turned neighbors into informants and people disappeared for telling the truth, keeping your mouth shut was the smart move.

And even today, for many in our community, that fear isn't just history—it's a Wednesday. When people are still being picked up, still disappearing into detention centers, still having their families torn apart, staying under the radar keeps families together.

After hours of exercises designed to flip your worldview upside down, something got jostled loose. I can't pinpoint what exactly triggered it; maybe it was one of those exercises that turned commonly held beliefs on their head, or someone else standing up to share their truth. All I know is that, suddenly, I was nine years old again.

The Morning My Family Unraveled

It was early morning, sometime around my ninth birthday, and the grass outside my bedroom window looked like a jigsaw of sunset shades of red and gold maple leaves blanketing our front yard like nature's attempt at comfort. Funny how clearly you remember the "before" of certain moments. On a normal morning, I might have heard my father's booming laugh echoing from the kitchen, or the familiar crackle of his sacred record player warming up with Bach or Beethoven. He could be so wonderfully silly, the kind of dad who'd let you ride on his back or who would break into spontaneous songs just to make you giggle.

My mom usually helped me get ready for school, but that morning, the soundtrack wasn't Bach or Beethoven from my father's record player. It was his rage. And my mother's cries. Both in Spanish. Both ricocheting through the walls like bullets.

My childhood was riddled with "Cállate" and "Déjame en paz," but that morning I heard "Sin vergüenza" and "¿Qué te pasa?"—words that cut deeper than the shouting ever could. They always argued in Spanish, the language of secrets. The language of "protection." Like switching tongues could somehow shield us from the meaning.

So, I dressed myself—stiff jean jacket, brown suede Hush Puppies, backpack over tiny shoulders—and mapped out my exit plan using skills I'd sharpened during neighborhood games of hide-and-seek. I knew I had to be careful because there was something different in my mother's voice that morning. Not just anger. Fear. Raw, unraveling fear. Something I'd never heard before. I reached the kitchen doorway. Their screams were so loud they wouldn't have heard me even if I hadn't tried to become air.

I paused in the opening and saw it: My father, arm raised high, holding an iron frying pan, about to swing. The same pan that made Sunday morning pancakes. The one whose weight I couldn't even lift. My mother was braced against the stove, one hand pressed flat on the coarse spiral burner to steady herself. Her back was arched. Her head turned. Her body frozen. Like a still photograph I can't forget.

He saw me.

His arm paused midair. We locked eyes.

All I could manage was a single word:

"Bye."

I turned, scrambled down the stairs, yanked the front door open, and ran.

I ducked behind the viburnum bush beside the garage, heart pounding against my ribs, stomach climbing into my throat. But mostly I felt relief. I was safe. For now.

A few minutes later, I heard the bus engine roar as it pulled away from my stop. I saw it pass in slow motion, feeling strange, like I was witnessing someone else's morning. Just like watching my father raise that frying pan had felt strange. Strange as in numb. Numb as in I felt nothing. I was out of my body. As if my feelings had gone into hiding too.

Then I heard keys. The jangle of metal. The click of the lock. My father opened the heavy front door and got behind the wheel of our powder-blue Chevy station wagon. He backed out of the driveway and drove off, following the same route as my bus.

And then it dawned on me. *What if she's dead?*

The thought crashed into me like a cold bucket of ice water. What if he'd killed her? What if that was why he left looking like nothing had happened? What if she was lying on the kitchen floor right now and I was the only one who knew?

My heart pounded. I stood frozen on the front steps, paralyzed but desperate to know if she was okay. What would I do if I found her? Who would I call? How do you explain something you're not supposed to have seen?

I nervously retraced my steps. Opened the front door. Each step up the stairs felt like walking toward the edge of a cliff. I made my way to the kitchen, holding my breath.

She was there. Still wearing her well-worn soft white nightgown with the faded pink flowers. Collapsed in a chair. Hands cupped over her face.

"Mom? Are you okay?"

She didn't answer. She just pressed her fingers deeper into her eyes, like she was trying to rub out the pain. Then she pulled me close. I stumbled forward to keep my balance. She wrapped her arms around my tiny torso and cried into my body. I wrapped my little nine-year-old arms around her and said, "It's going to be okay, Mom."

A week later, everything felt different but looked exactly the same. I went to school, ate my cereal, did my homework, but underneath it all was this burden I carried alone. The secret wrapped itself around my heart, making everything feel heavy and fragile at the same time.

My fourth-grade teacher handed me a thick stack of worksheets and told me to gather all my things and bring them to the office. The manila envelope felt important in my hands, official somehow. I walked down the hall, and my rubber-soled sneakers scuffed against that low-pile carpet that covered the whole school. Across the courtyard, I spotted my brother David doing the same thing—clutching his own stack of papers, looking confused as hell.

That's when it registered, like a movie playing behind my eyes: the frying pan, my father, my mother bent over the stove. Suddenly I understood what was happening.

He'd almost killed her. And now we were leaving.

When my mom walked into the office, I could tell she'd been crying. She never took off her circa 1970s oversized prescription sunglasses and darted around the office like she was running out of time. David kept asking questions in the car, spiraling with his unmedicated ADHD energy. But I stayed calm. I was outside my body again, watching from a distance. Numb and floating above the uncertainty. The way children learn to survive moments they shouldn't have to face.

We flew to San Juan, Puerto Rico, where my only living abuela lived, on a postage-stamp-sized island in the Caribbean where the seasons never changed and love came con ganas—with freshly sliced pineapple every morning, hands that smoothed my hair while I slept, and a certainty that I was the most precious thing that ever existed. We would stay until Daddy got "his anger problem under control." As if rage were something you could fix in four weeks and putting an ocean between us would somehow heal what was damaged between them.

This wasn't just a hard chapter of my childhood; it was the moment my nervous system learned to keep the peace by staying ready for anything. For years, it shaped how I showed up in conflict, in leadership, and in love. Like an invisible force guiding every decision.

That morning, I entered into an unspoken contract with the world: Keep it together. Keep it quiet. Keep it moving, because invisible kids don't get hurt.

And there I was, decades later, sitting in that Miami Beach ballroom where this memory had first broken through. It was strange how it surfaced—not like discovering something new, but like finally looking directly at something that had always been there, dangling in the periphery of my mind.

Familiar but blurry. Like something I'd walked past every day but never acknowledged, never looked at long enough to understand. And since I couldn't share it with anyone, I couldn't process it. I could only sit with it by myself, trying to make sense of something that felt beyond my ability to understand.

But at least I'd allowed it into my consciousness, where it would stay for decades, waiting.

I couldn't unsee it now. The memory felt like a movie I'd watched but couldn't quite believe was my own life. I knew it was too significant to ignore, but I couldn't put my finger on how.

Therapists call it a psychological milestone, something that leaves a lasting emotional and personal imprint that then shapes your identity. I call it the day my childhood decided to take early retirement.

Something about what happened that morning was driving me and shaping my choices in ways I couldn't yet understand.

I didn't just witness violence that day. I stepped into a role I hadn't chosen: protector, peacekeeper, silent observer. The holy trinity of trauma responses. My voice could stop violence, but speaking up felt riskier than staying quiet. I became expert at reading rooms, absorbing tension, smoothing over conflicts before they erupted. I thought I was just being a good daughter. I didn't notice I was training myself to be a professional secret keeper. I didn't know those roles I'd taken on would follow me into adulthood disguised as work ethic, ambition, and loyalty.

The pattern followed me everywhere.

In relationships, I swallowed my needs to keep the peace. In my career, I said yes to everything and asked for little or nothing in return. Every project, every favor, every impossible deadline—yes, yes, yes. The corporate game never made sense to me, so I defaulted to what had helped me win as a daughter: overgiving.

For years, the memory just lived there on the periphery. I told my husband, Kevin, about it, but it never felt urgent enough for therapy. It wasn't as if I were having nightmares or panic attacks. It was more like having a splinter in your foot you can feel but can't quite reach, even with tweezers. You change how you walk, just enough to avoid the pain, even if it throws everything else out of alignment.

I could see how that morning had shaped me. The hypervigilance. The desire to keep people I loved safe. The way I read rooms. But understanding it and knowing what to do about it were completely different things.

It stayed there, impossible to ignore.

The Framework That Showed Me Who I Thought I Was

Years earlier, a Latina graduate student in Marshall Ganz's Harvard class had used my film as an example of Story of Us—the shared values that unite a community. She'd reached out to tell me how the film had impacted her understanding of first-generation identity, planting seeds for me to understand how important this work was and making me curious about Marshall himself.

We flew from Denver to Boston to interview him for a follow-up project. In the sixties Marshall had left Harvard to work alongside César Chávez and Dolores Huerta for sixteen years, helping build the United Farm Workers movement from the ground up. Decades later, he brought those same organizing principles to President Obama's 2008 campaign, where his storytelling approach helped create unprecedented grassroots momentum.

Before we even started the formal interview, something wildly uncommon happened. Marshall turned the tables and started interviewing me, and like an expert interviewer he somehow got a story out of me. This was different from the usual pre-interview small talk. From everything I'd researched about him and the short amount of time we'd spent together that morning, I could tell our conversation would be pivotal. I had an intuitive feeling he had something that could help me understand what I'd been carrying all these years.

That's when I shared the frying pan story.

"You saved her life that morning," he said, after I'd finished. "And now you're trying to save the world."

The words knocked the wind out of me. Because he was right. My entire adult life—my career choices, my relationships, my relentless drive to help others—was all connected to that nine-year-old girl who believed her voice was powerful enough to protect her mother.

Marshall explained that we don't change the world through statistics or arguments. We move it through story. Through connecting our personal experiences to our shared values, and then to the urgent challenges of our time. His Public Narrative framework revolves around three elements: a Story of Self, which reveals the values that called you to action; a Story of Us, which identifies the values we share; and a Story of Now, which presents an urgent challenge we must face together.

For the first time, I had language for what I'd been feeling but couldn't articulate. The framework gave me permission to see my story as part of a larger reality and my healing as part of a larger solution. I knew I had to start sharing the frying pan story publicly. I had to stop treating my childhood trauma like a shameful secret and start seeing it as my Story of Self—the moment that revealed my core value: using my voice to create safety.

I started sharing my Story of Self when it made sense—with close friends, and even in my coaching calls when a client was struggling with their own origin story. Instead of keeping the frying pan story locked away like something that disqualified me, I began offering it as a bridge to understanding.

The first time I shared it without that familiar weight of shame, I felt something change. I wasn't protecting it anymore—I was using it as a tool. And I could feel something that had been frozen for decades warming up.

Marshall had given me the language—Story of Self—but what I was discovering went deeper than his framework. I was learning something about what happens when we stop keeping certain things locked away behind closed doors. Each time I chose to share that story, I was opening the door wider, allowing warmth to flow back to a place I'd abandoned.

The story wasn't my burden anymore—it became my foundation.

The women showing up at the film screenings, sharing their own stories of being caught between worlds—they were my Story of Us. And I had to help them see we shared something deeper than just first-gen struggles. Our collective secrecy about family trauma was the urgent Story of Now that we needed to face together—because that secrecy was keeping us from claiming our dreams, our voices, and our power. That's why I'm sharing the frying pan story with you here in these pages. Because if Marshall was right, if we can change the world through story, then this is how we start.

But more than that, it helped me understand that liberation isn't just personal, it's collective. When we break free from the patterns that keep us small, we inspire others to do the same. This approach to healing reflects what we value most as a culture. Even when we fall short, the aspiration is clear: We don't pull ourselves up by our bootstraps and leave everyone else behind. When we heal, we heal together.

What Marshall shared stayed with me. It took time to fully absorb, but once it did, it became foundational to my work on stage. I have this unexplainable desire to be what Michelle Obama once called "a woman of consequence." I heard her say this at her first live public appearance after leaving the White House, and something clicked inside me. I want to live a consequential life, to leave something meaningful behind. Maybe this yearning explains how that morning shaped me.

When you witness something that significant, and don't have words to speak about it, it creates this . . . pressure. Like you have to do something important with your life to justify carrying that weight.

The residue left a relentless desire to make a big impact, to prove that surviving that moment meant something.

I packed it away, the way we all do. I could see it there, I knew it existed, but I still didn't know how to carry it. This drive to have a big life that both fuels and exhausts me.

In my late twenties, I'd started working on a documentary film that had been incubating for seventeen years. By my early forties, I was collaborating with Academy Award nominee Henry Ansbacher on *being eñye*—a film about the lived experience of first-generation American-born Latinos who felt caught between two identities.

The film was about that space between worlds—never fully belonging to your parents' country, never fully accepted in your own. There was a common thread among first-generation Americans that I wanted to validate, a story I wanted to bring forth. At the time, there was nothing like it.

When I interviewed my father's best friend, Tony, for the film, we set up in his backyard, the same one I'd spent countless hours in as a kid. His house was just two doors down from where I grew up, and sitting there with the camera rolling felt like stepping back in time. Tony and his wife, Erika, had been fixtures in our neighborhood and an essential part of the fabric of my childhood.

After we wrapped up the formal interview, the cameras were off and we were just sitting there in the familiar space of their backyard, talking the way neighbors that have become like family do. That's when he said something that stopped me cold. . . .

"Remember when I took you guys to the airport when you were a little girl? When your mom took you and David to Puerto Rico?"

My heart stopped. He didn't know about the violence that morning; my brothers weren't there to see it either. But Tony had witnessed something else, the leaving. He drove us to the airport because my mom needed someone to bring the car back home. That whole piece I'd forgotten completely.

For years, part of me had wondered if I'd imagined it all. If trauma had twisted a normal fight into something more dramatic in my nine-year-old mind. But Tony's casual mention confirmed it; something significant enough had happened to make my mother flee to Puerto Rico with two small children. For a month.

I had a corroborator. The memory was real.

Still, it would be another year or two before I'd find the courage to share it publicly. But that moment with Tony is when it stopped being a question mark and became a period. The harm I'd witnessed, the secret I'd carried, the role I'd stepped into as family protector, it had actually happened.

It would take me decades and a documentary film to finally understand how to break free from the weight of that morning.

Telling My Story

When it came time to share my own story on camera in the film, I was a wreck.

The day we recorded it, we were supposed to be interviewing one of my idols, Maria Hinojosa, but she needed the time to prep for a TEDx Talk and unfortunately had to cancel the night before. So instead of heading to Harlem, we went to the graveyard where my father and brother are buried—just me, Henry Ansbacher (my coproducer and codirector), and our devoted camera guy, Freddie.

It was an overcast and muggy summer day and I was spent. We'd been shooting in New York for almost ten days straight. Freddie was futzing with the audio, which he could not get to work, and I was in a shit mood. I shared that I thought it was a sign and that maybe this scene wasn't meant to be. I didn't want to be there. I didn't want to be in the graveyard. I didn't want to tell this story. I thought the audio not working would be enough reason to call it a day, but right when we were about to shut everything down, miraculously it began to work, so we proceeded.

I didn't think sharing the deaths would make any difference. I didn't see a connection between how their deaths shaped my identity and what we were trying to do with the film.

The truth is, I never wanted to include this scene. Henry pushed for it, and I fought him on it tooth and nail. What did my father's death have to do with a film about Latino identity?

What I couldn't see was that I wasn't just grieving his death, I was grieving an unfinished story. After that morning with the frying pan, my father did the hardest thing a person can do: He changed. He found God, joined a men's support group, and got his rage under control. I had a front-row seat to watch someone fight their demons and win, and we were happier as a family because of it.

He became my hero.

And then, he died.

Just when I thought I knew how his story would unfold, it was over, and I was left holding all the complicated pieces. The violent man, the man he became, the father I adored, and the story that would never get its proper ending.

I didn't want to share that on camera because I hated being pitied. And this felt like the kind of story that invited exactly that.

I realized later that grief cracks everything open. When a parent dies, all your cultural conditioning shows up—how you mourn, what you're allowed to say, whom you're expected to protect. And what stories we are allowed to tell about someone whom we loved and feared at the same time.

But life is complex and layered, and this scene illustrated that many factors contribute to how a person feels about who they are in the world, and where and why they belong.

Shooting this moment at the foot of the graves made me feel exposed in a way that made my skin crawl. I was convinced no one would care. That it was self-indulgent.

On camera, I'm sitting at my father's grave talking about how his death impacted me, and I get really upset, embarrassingly upset.

Watching it back, later, with the editors, I kept questioning myself. . . .

Why would I choose to bring up this old family pain? Why couldn't I just be over losing my father at thirteen, like a "normal" person?

Sitting there in that editing suite, one question haunted me: Was I honoring him, or just reopening old wounds? These weren't just artistic questions; they were cultural taboos speaking.

The very act of making the film felt like breaking a sacred covenant. Not just with my family, but with generations of women who'd been taught that protection meant staying silent, that love meant keeping secrets, and that loyalty meant never telling the world what really happened behind closed doors. Whether it was an attempted murder by frying pan, a tragic death, or any of the other events that weighed on my subconscious.

As we worked through the rough cut of the film for the next thirty-seven minutes, I sat paralyzed, barely able to watch my most vulnerable moments play out on screen.

Something deeper was driving me forward. Maybe it was that nine-year-old girl who had found her voice in a moment of crisis, or Marshall's words constantly swimming in my mind, or maybe I was just exhausted from carrying secrets that were never mine to keep. I couldn't know it then, sitting in that editing room, but choosing myself wasn't choosing against my family.

I didn't see how my truth would become someone else's invitation to be free. Once we started showing the film, people weren't thanking me for being brave, they were thanking me for showing them what was possible when you stop editing yourself to death.

The graveyard scene I'd almost cut to avoid being pitied has been brought up countless times. "When you talked about your father," one woman said, "I felt like you were talking about mine." She had lost her father as a teenager too. "Nobody prepared me for how losing him would reshape everything about our family." My vulnerability had become a doorway for others.

It took experiencing this reaction over and over, with different audiences, different generations, different nationalities, before I understood something crucial—the things I was most afraid to share were the things people appreciated the most.

This became the pattern at every screening that followed, and still, years later, it continues after every keynote I give. After the lights come up or I step off the stage, what I now call "the line of secrets and dreams" forms. People wait, sometimes for hours, to share things they've never told anyone out loud and dreams they've never dared to pursue. The woman who wants to quit her job and start a speaking business but feels selfish—as if she's asking for too much when she should be grateful where she is. The higher education administrator who wants to write a book about her incarcerated mother but doesn't dare until her mom dies. The new mother who wants to make a documentary, inspired by my story, grapples with mom guilt instead.

Whether I'm talking about the film or speaking about belonging, identity, and finding your voice, the result is the same. Something in my vulnerability seems to stir something long-buried. They start sharing truths they've kept silent for years, family secrets, personal dreams, stories they believed would make them unlovable.

Every sleepless night I'd spent agonizing over whether to include something, every moment I'd considered editing out a difficult truth to spare someone's feelings, those were the exact moments that created the deepest connections.

I started to understand that my instinct for self-preservation was actually a form of self-sabotage. By trying to shield everyone from my truth, I was robbing them of the chance to feel less alone in theirs.

Months later, at an event hosted by the Federal Reserve Bank of New York, what struck me was that telling the real story can also transform careers.

Walking past armed security and through full-body metal detectors to screen a documentary about Latino identity felt surreal. But after the formal screening and Q&A, the space was transformed into a joyful celebration—live music, dancing, the most impeccably catered Puerto Rican spread I'd ever experienced. It was like they'd imported a block party into one of the most secure buildings in Manhattan.

And then, inevitably, it happened again. I had just sat down at a high-top table to catch my breath from dancing when two women in elegant black cocktail dresses approached me. They were clearly successful Latina professionals, the kind of women who belonged in rooms such as this, confident and refined but super down-to-earth. You could tell they were used to commanding respect, but there was something warm and approachable about them too.

Without any prompting, they started sharing their stories with me, the same topics that always came up wherever I went: domestic violence, sexual assault, mental health struggles, addiction, all the things our community doesn't talk about and that we're supposed to find a way to just "get over." But these women weren't just speaking from pain; they were speaking from insight. They understood the cultural code of protection, the taboos that made sure they stayed hidden.

What struck me was how they connected it all—how growing up navigating what we could and couldn't say about our families had trained us to self-silence professionally too. The same instinct that keeps us hushed about trauma at home keeps us from speaking up in boardrooms, from negotiating boldly, from taking up space as leaders.

As they shared, I watched their faces—the relief of finally saying it out loud mixed with the yearning of needing someone else to help them find a way forward. They weren't just asking me to address trauma; they were asking me to help break the cultural patterns that were holding all of us back. And then came the question that would redirect my entire focus: "Would you ever consider doing something about this? For our community?"

Standing there, listening to them, it dawned on me that I'd been preparing for this moment my whole life. Every woman who'd whispered her secrets to me, every time I'd felt the weight of cultural restraint, it was all leading here. This wasn't just about my trauma anymore; it was about transforming how we handle it as a community. Maybe navigating my own family's taboos had given me the tools to help other women break theirs.

The proof was already there: that nine-year-old girl who walked into the kitchen and said, "Bye." Who saved her mother's life by being a human pattern interrupt.

The change wasn't just about making the film. It was about understanding that the very thing I'd been most afraid to share—my truth, my vulnerability, my story—could actually be my greatest gift. Not just to me, but to others.

But what would it look like to expand this? How do you take what happens on the line of "secrets and dreams" and turn it into something that could shift our entire community's relationship with power?

I would have to go even deeper and fight harder to find the answer.

She sees herself as an agent of change.

Reflection: Make Art

Last summer while my family and I were on vacation in Lisbon, a friend suggested a mosaic class she thought we'd love. She was right. My girls and I spent three hours sitting around a huge square table in a light-filled art studio, arranging tiny pieces of colored tile in the shape of a fish while music fueled our creativity—a playlist curated from years of past student requests. There was something healing about taking broken, jagged pieces of tile and rearranging them until they made sense. Until they made something beautiful.

The whole experience was dreamy. We laughed and shared stories with a Scottish couple sitting across from us at our table, and we connected with our instructor, who had the most romantic story—an American who'd come to Portugal on business, fallen in love with both the country and her future husband, and completely reinvented herself as a mosaic artist and teacher.

When I asked the girls what the highlight of the trip was, this class won hands down.

You know those moments when you pat yourself on the back for making a good decision? That was this.

As you begin this journey of reclaiming your story and getting liberated, I want you to remember something: *You deserve time spent like this.* You deserve joy for no other reason than that you exist.

Making art, whether it's painting by numbers as my girls and I did during the pandemic, writing an essay, taking any kind of craft class, or, yes, making a short film about your community, gives your heart somewhere safe and soft to land while you're doing this deeper work. Your truth will come rushing forward!

Here's your invitation: While you're reading this book, make something. Anything. Let your hands create while your heart heals.

What will you make?

CHAPTER TWO

De Eso No Se Habla:

How to Speak the Unspeakable to the World

Every Latina knows the exact moment she realizes she's not Latina enough. Mine happened at thirty thousand feet somewhere over Pennsylvania.

I was staring out of the airplane window, watching the lights below blur together, when it registered that in less than twenty-four hours some hundred-odd people would be watching my documentary. Not just any film, but one that had somehow shifted from being about 16 million first-generation Latinos to being about me.

Our Southwest flight touched down that afternoon in January at LaGuardia, and it was already dark and cold as hell in New York City. Walking near Henry's aunt's Upper West Side town house, trying not to slip on the ice, I felt anxiety completely take over my body. The film was supposed to be about the others, but somehow it had become about me—*about them but through me*—and I just couldn't get my head around that idea. Mostly because I was already dealing with my own crap around being Latina enough and just . . . worthy enough, in general. At the time I believed that my "faults," all the ways I'd failed to be a "good Latina," were exactly why the film shouldn't be about me. Henry felt strongly that those were exactly why I'd be perfect.

What the ever-loving hell was he thinking?

Henry said that so many people would be able to identify once they heard my story. So, after some soul searching, I chose to trust him, and my story, which we told together.

At times the film project felt bigger than both of us. I agreed to coproducing it, being interviewed for it, and codirecting it alongside him.

Screening it felt like another thing entirely. It's like the difference between being pregnant and having the baby and then, in this case, not wanting anyone to hold the baby—ever.

It was just too personal.

I didn't expect the panic that emerged when I thought about strangers seeing it. And I know that's got to sound weird. The closer we got to finishing and to this screening in New York, the more reluctant I began to feel. I had desperately wanted to make the film for so many years that the only thing I thought about while working on it was simply getting it done.

But now it *was* done, and we were about to show it, and I was spiraling. What had I been thinking? A hundred people were going to sit there and watch me spill my guts, judge my story, maybe even misunderstand my family. I felt too exposed and, then later, I felt sick with regret.

My ego, on the other hand, loved being the central character.

When the cameras rolled on me, I felt like a star. The attention felt phenomenal, and the daily blowouts took it to a new level. Not long before, I was a stay-at-home mom who wasn't showering regularly and wore my hair in a moño. Now, I was a part of production meetings, interviewing celebrities, staying in hotels, and walking up Fifth Avenue in the Puerto Rican Day Parade with camera guys surrounding me to get the perfect shot.

And while I recognize that I just told you I'd already granted my consent and made a conscious decision to trust, there was a clear disconnect in my mind between what it felt like to make the film (amazing) and what it felt like once we were done (super scary).

But that night on the sidewalk, panicking about the screening, I found myself opening up about things I'd long kept private. Henry, my creative partner on the film, has a degree in counseling, and since that first pitch meeting in his office in Denver two years prior, I'd always found myself comfortable talking to him about most anything. Curious about how I was feeling, he asked a few questions and suddenly I was gushing out all kinds of sadness while the bitter cold New York City air was burning through my nose and into my throat. A gust of wind off the Hudson cut through my coat and froze the sweat running down my back. My feet slipped around on the icy pavement as I tried to explain the cruelness of pity. The sidewalk felt unstable beneath me, like it could no longer support the weight of my self-doubt.

We'd gone out to dinner right around the corner from the house, but I barely touched my food. The whole time I was figuring out how to tell Henry I believed we'd made a huge mistake, or at least I had.

"I'm sorry, Henry. I just can't."

"Can't what, Denise?"

"I can't let people see it tomorrow night. I've revealed way too much."

Back at his aunt's place, we ended up in the rustic kitchen, my favorite room in that big house with its worn wooden table and mismatched chairs. Something about that space made me feel safe enough to spill everything I'd been holding back.

I told him about Kevin and me selling our wedding rings to pay bills. About our car getting repossessed.

And I shared that if the screening the following night wasn't a complete success, then I would feel like an absolute idiot and the sacrifices would have been for naught, and frankly I couldn't bear that level of failure.

Wiping the tears from my now-swollen eyes, I became aware of how much I'd shared.

With both palms flat on the table I pushed myself up. "Now you know everything, and now I feel powerless."

My body turned away from him as I began to walk into the darkness of the next room.

He reached toward me with his arm outstretched. "Powerless? Denise, you know your power is not derived from what you choose to withhold, right?"

I shut him down with some sarcastic response. But inside I was still crumbling. I'd crossed a cultural line and shared my family's dirty laundry. And for what?

I'd betrayed my family and my culture, and the following night I would pay the price. In twenty-four hours, I'd still be a stay-at-home mom but I'd also be a failure who chose to blow through $50,000 in savings chasing some stupid dream instead of putting it toward a house like a responsible adult.

What the hell had I done? I was totally screwed.

Learning to Trust What Scares You Most

Leaving my room on my way to brush my teeth, my bare feet melted into the thick red velvety carpet in the hall—such a contrast from the hardwood floor of my room. Morning light burst through the original Tiffany glass skylight above me and I couldn't help but feel inspired. Something so delicate and beautiful, thoughtfully positioned above five sturdy floors of mahogany and stone. It struck me how fragile beauty could anchor an entire house, just as the vulnerable story we were about to share would anchor this entire evening.

"It's going to be okay, Denise. You're going to be okay."

Your power is not derived from what you choose to withhold.

I didn't buy it. Not really. Every part of me was screaming that secrets are meant to be kept, that sharing them would only bring negative consequences. But something gave way in that moment. Not belief exactly, but maybe . . . willingness? Like maybe I could consider the possibility that he wasn't completely wrong.

The reality was, there was no backing out now. We'd committed to these people, to this event, to this whole thing. I'd painted myself into a corner so completely that the only way out was through. And maybe that's how the impossible stuff happens, when you cut off every exit and force yourself to figure it out.

I recognized I had to untether myself from the old identity that believed if I put myself this far out there, I might die. I had to be willing to evolve, to transcend who I thought I was. It felt like an ego death, like stepping into an emotional birth canal.

Sometimes that's what growth requires, complete surrender to becoming someone new.

If this was going to fail, at least I'd know I gave it everything. That was better than holding back and always wondering, *What if?*

In the next several years, on stages across the country, the truth revealed itself time and time again. The more vulnerable I was willing to be, the more powerful the connection.

If you're building a brand, leading a team, speaking, creating content—pay attention to this. People can smell sanitized stories from a mile away. They're not looking for your curated life; they're starving for something real.

This doesn't mean trauma dumping in the boardroom. It means sharing the real challenges you've overcome, the lessons from your actual experiences, the perspective that comes from your unique journey. So, when you're presenting to leadership or building trust with your team, those authentic moments that convey "Here's what I learned when I had to navigate this difficult situation" are what create real connection and show your value.

I know this feels risky when you're already the "only" Latina in the room. But allow me to be the first person to remind you today that your lived experiences aren't liabilities to hide, they're strategic assets that set you apart.

Learning to trust my intuition became one of my proudest accomplishments as an adult. For years, I couldn't tell the difference between my voice and what I thought people wanted me to say.

After the first few screenings, I kept bracing for the crash. Every time someone responded with tears or thanks or said, "You told my story," I convinced myself it was a fluke. This time they would walk out. This time someone would call me out. This time they would see the film wasn't actually that good.

I was still running on that old software: not good enough, who do you think you are, don't get too confident. I couldn't accept what was happening right in front of me. I had made something that touched people. I had turned my pain into art that healed others. And maybe, just maybe, that meant I was good too.

But something else was happening at these screenings that I hadn't expected. True to Latino form, communities weren't just showing the film; they were creating entire events around it. Screenings became receptions. Receptions became dinners. I'd end up meeting with mayors, community leaders, activists. Our magnificent ability to build community around storytelling was on full display.

And in every single one of these spaces, a pattern emerged.

Didn't matter if I was in New York or Virginia, Minnesota or New Mexico, Texas or California. After the lights went up, people wanted to talk about the same things. The deeper things. The secrets. The taboos I hadn't dared to include in the film.

Which made me wonder: If it had been so scary for me to share what I *did* share, and people were hungry to go so much deeper . . . what was I still hiding from?

These post-screening conversations stunned me, not just because of how intense they were, but how predictable. People I'd never met across the country were voicing the *same pain*. They were ready to excavate their own buried stories. It was as if I'd given them permission to start digging.

But I was still playing it safe. Still protecting everyone, including myself, from the whole truth.

That changed at screening #44.

Screening #44: LinkedIn HQ

My Spanx were already betraying me. They sat right below my bra, and I'd been in them for hours. The rolling-down-from-the-top feeling had commenced and I had to stand a certain way to make sure they stayed put.

Two hundred and fifty people were packed into LinkedIn's headquarters that night in downtown San Francisco. Standing room only. My favorite coral-red dress clung differently now, my body still adjusting to life on the road. Airport meals with too much sodium, too many missed workouts, and a schedule that never seemed to pause. My spine prickled. The jean jacket stayed on. Not because the air-conditioning was too high. But because I kept hearing that voice: *Your arms are too big. Too jiggly. These people expect a put-together speaker, not someone who looks like she's been living on airport pretzels.*

Forty-three screenings before this one. You'd think I'd be used to it by now. The stages. The lights. The questions. God, the questions, they were always my favorite part. Electric with possibility. But still, my stomach would twist. Still wondered if I would be enough. Nervous I couldn't be who they needed me to be up there.

All I wanted was to make it through the thirty minutes and to get to that glass of vino waiting backstage. Escape before someone asked something I wasn't ready to answer.

The irony wasn't lost on me. Here I was, in Silicon Valley's shrine to professional success, about to shatter the one thing nobody talks about in corporate America. About to break the cardinal rule of cardinal rules . . .

Keep your messy personal life out of the workplace.

Each person who stepped up to the microphone tore down another piece of that perfect professional facade. The way they opened up before even asking their questions, raw, honest, and so damn brave. It took my breath away. Something powerful was unfolding in that sterile corporate space.

And then, he raised his hand.

No polite walk to the microphone line in the back of the room. He raised his hand from where he was sitting. Tall, lanky, brown skin, pressed shirt, humble. Cute. His presence commanded attention.

Someone passed him a microphone. I felt my Spanx squeeze tighter. And then he stood up.

In a New York accent he said, "I know where you grew up. I know this isn't the whole story. It can't be. What did you leave out?"

What the ever-loving f kind of question is that? That was my first thought.

My second: *Don't cry.*

Right there, in the middle of LinkedIn HQ, in front of 250 of the Bay Area's highest-achieving Latino professionals, I remembered something that helped me answer him.

I'd been at a speaker training not long before this, and on the final day, I asked the annoyingly slick lead instructor to share a hard moment from onstage and what he'd learned. I wasn't trying to trip him up, I just wanted something real. Everything about this conference had felt overproduced and fake. He looked straight at me and said he wasn't going to answer my question.

Seriously? He's not going to answer me?

I lost every ounce of respect I had for him in the time it took him to say no. I remember thinking, *Never be that guy.*

And that's when I made a decision. If I was ever in that same situation, I would answer the effing question. I would meet the moment with the truth because that was a million times better than being known for being a come mierda, which is exactly how I saw him from that point on.

Tell the truth, no matter what.

Looking back at everything that has happened in the almost ten years since then, I see that's where this whole story began.

Now it was my turn.

I looked straight at the young man who'd asked the question, but I felt the eyes of every person in that room wondering, just as I was, if they were about to hear something real or some sanitized bullshit.

My nose started tingling, which is the first sign of one of my emotional waves. Tears began to well up and faces blurred. I worried whether my lash glue would hold.

Breathe, Denise. Breathe, I told myself, scanning the room one last time.

The room went dead silent. The handheld mic in my right hand felt as if it weighed a hundred pounds. My thumb slid over the ridge that could shut it down with a single click. My Spanx were putting a vise grip on my torso, squeezing the air out like they were giving me one last chance to bail on the moment completely.

And then, I did what I do best when I'm nervous: I overshared.

"I left out that I was raped my freshman year of college." *Breathe.*

"I left out that I once saw my father almost kill my mother in a fight over breakfast when I was nine." *Breathe.*

"I left out the parts I thought would make you turn away. The things we're taught to bury so deep they become part of who we are instead of what happened to us. But what I didn't understand, not until after the film came out, was that those are the stories that matter most."

And just like that, I wasn't hot anymore.

Nobody moved. The people who were headed to the bathroom were frozen midstep. Time stood still in that way it does when someone says the thing everyone's been thinking but no one's been brave enough to just say.

The moment those words left my mouth, you could hear a pin drop. All eyes were on me, and I felt absolutely naked up there. But I also knew, instantly, that this was helping. They were hungry for something authentic, and I was serving up raw honesty.

I could feel the energy shift in my body, and that pressure you feel as a speaker when something isn't landing suddenly dissipated. People leaned forward. Phones went away. In a standing-room-only crowd, everyone just . . . stopped and listened. Some were crying—

not because they were uncomfortable, but because they were moved to tears.

The Q&A ran forty minutes over because the line to the microphone kept growing. And afterward, I walked offstage and found a line of people waiting to talk to me. They wanted to share their secrets, just as I had. One after another, they told me their truths: sexual assaults, domestic violence, family shame, dreams they'd buried because they didn't think they were allowed to want them.

One person after another told me the same thing: It felt real. It became evident people didn't care about perfection; they yearned for something genuine. And when you show up as yourself, you give them permission to do the same.

It wasn't just about telling the truth publicly. It was about breaking the spell of suppression that had been passed down through generations of de eso no se habla. But that night, we *did* talk about it.

And the talking set us free.

This wasn't trauma dumping. I'd been on forty-three stages before this one. I knew the difference between confessing and sharing from power. I wasn't unloading on them; I was showing them that our scars—and the stories about how we survived them—could become sources of strength.

That night it became painfully obvious that when you speak the truth, yes, some people get uncomfortable and back away. But the right people lean in. They've been waiting for someone to go first so they can finally exhale and share what they've been carrying. That's how real leadership works: not by pretending you never struggled, but by showing how you got through the struggle.

All those years I thought keeping everything inside was protecting me. But playing it safe was just making me smaller and smaller until I could barely recognize myself.

Oversharing wasn't my problem. Overcensoring was. So many of us are walking around pretending we're fine when we're not, and calling that "professional" or "appropriate." But what if the real problem isn't our messy truths, but that we've all agreed to hide them?

And I was *so* done with hiding.

The Healing Power of Witnesses

The private work I'd done in therapy had saved me because it gave me the tools to function, to rebuild, to keep going. But that night, sharing the truth in front of an audience who received it with grace, not judgment, healed me in a way nothing else ever had.

Because shame withers when it's met with compassion.

When I spoke those words out loud and saw people nod instead of recoil, something that had haunted me for decades finally died. Not just for me, but for every other person in that room carrying their own hidden story.

The next two years were a blur. Opportunities came flying in: invitations, events, flights between Denver and the Bay Area. Companies wanted the film, the story, and the conversation.

But professional opportunities aside, what changed most was my understanding of authenticity's true power. I learned that when we're called to share publicly, when that gut feeling tells us it's time, being as authentic as we can possibly be doesn't just help others, it completes our own healing.

I never shared those two specific truths publicly again. I didn't need to. That one moment of complete honesty—that choice to trust my intuition over what I'd been taught—had done what it needed to do. It wasn't about making those stories part of my regular repertoire. It was about proving to myself that I could choose authenticity over being guarded when it mattered most.

Manifesto: The Difference Between Private and Public Truth

Our culture's obsession with appearances—el qué dirán—isn't just about reputation. It's about control. It's about keeping generations of women in check through the currency of shame. And every time we choose avoidance to dodge judgment, we reinforce the taboos that have kept us small.

But there's a difference between telling your therapist about your trauma and telling a roomful of people. Both are necessary, but they serve different purposes.

Private truth telling heals *you.*

Public truth telling heals *the culture.*

When we keep our healing private, we miss the chance to break the cycle for others who are still trapped in the same isolation that once held us.

I want you to know that you should never feel obligated to share your private pain publicly. Your healing is yours, and it can stay yours forever if that's what serves you. Only you get to decide when, or if, you're ready to share it.

For me, it became impossible to hold back. After hundreds of stages and as many conversations, I kept hearing the same stories, the same pain, the same isolation. Woman after woman would approach me and say some version of "I thought I was the only one who felt this way." It became clear—I had to help break these cycles, to show others they weren't alone. Not from obligation, but because bearing witness changed me, and I couldn't go back.

And I don't want to pass that shit down.

You, my new friend, get to choose. There's no pressure from me, only space for you to make that decision. I do want you to feel safe telling your story, whether that's in therapy, to your best friend, or from a stage someday.

The choice is always yours.

Secrecy isn't our strength; it's tradition, and it's passed down like my cousin Lourdes's arroz con gandules recipe, only seasoned with silence and de eso no se habla.

Secrets might feel as if they're protecting us, but concealment moves through your body like a slow poison. Trust me, I know. I spent years swallowing words that needed to be spoken, thinking I was shielding everyone. But I was protecting everyone from truth, from healing, from the possibility that speaking might actually set us all free.

This book is about what happens when we stop buying the lie that secrets keep us safe.

The Power of Public Truth

When we start asking what (and whom) our censoring is really protecting, we discover the cost of cherry-picking our truth and editing ourselves down to what's comfortable for everyone else but us. This is about telling the whole damn story. Even when the people around us might not be ready. It took me decades to learn we (you and me) are the only ones who ever need to be ready.

But there's a difference between private processing and public truth telling. I'd spent years in therapy working through my trauma—the rape, witnessing domestic violence as a child. That healing was mine, and it served its purpose. But when that guy at LinkedIn asked what I'd left out of my story, I saw clearly that the audience needed honesty.

In a room of 250 people, statistically 62 had experienced sexual assault. They didn't need to hear I was strong. They needed to see that surviving and thriving was possible. They needed to know they weren't alone in their exact lived experience.

The words hung in the air for what felt like forever, then I felt the room exhale. Afterward, they shared everything, their own experiences, their fears, their gratitude, stories they'd been told weren't "appropriate" for work. Because it's true what they say about shame: It can't survive in the light.

This is why truth telling from stages matters. Because when someone says the unspoken part out loud, when someone finally shares that you can carry trauma *and* still make it to big stages, still follow your dreams, still refuse to let one night in 1988 define your entire life, it creates space. It reminds us we're not alone, we're not damaged, and we don't have to choose between our healing and our dreams.

Secrets don't protect anyone.

They isolate us, make us feel alone in our pain and rob us of the connections that can heal us. The stories we're most afraid to tell, the ones that make us feel exposed, are often the very stories that need to be told. Not because we owe anyone our trauma, but because speaking them out loud breaks the spell of shame.

And sometimes, that act of truth telling doesn't just set us free. It becomes the key to someone else's freedom too.

But it's not easy to uncover the secrets, reckon with them, and find closure. I had three phases before I reconciled with mine.

Phase 1: Create Your Container

Find your most trusted space, whether that's with a therapist, a dear friend, your favorite prima that you can tell anything to, or your spouse. For me, it was Henry's documentary setup with one crucial agreement: I could share everything first and decide what to keep in the film later. The key is having complete control and agency over your story. Share it all in that safe space, reflect and evaluate later.

Phase 2: Find Your Filter

Don't try to sort through your story in its raw form. I refused to watch my interviews until they were edited into scenes. Let your brain trust reflect back the power and beauty in what feels messy to you. Maybe that's your therapist helping you reframe your narrative, your best friend pointing out your strengths when all you see is struggle, or your mentor showing you how your experience is actually your competitive advantage. Sometimes we need distance and skilled hands to help us understand what we've lived through.

Phase 3: Trust Your Truth

When I finally saw my story crafted into scenes, I could feel its power immediately. I was hesitant, but I could also sense the genuine excitement in Henry and the editing team. They weren't just doing a job; they were moved by what we'd all created. That's when I remembered what I told myself as a little girl, that my painful experiences would somehow help people when I was older.

The truth is, when we share authentically from the heart, it has the power to deepen relationships and change hearts and minds. It has more power than forcing something ever could.

This chapter is where the unraveling began, where I first understood that staying small was never about safety. I'm not here to survive anymore.

And neither are you.

She chooses authenticity over protection.

Reflection: Your Secret Weapon

Let's try something:

Write down the story you're most afraid to share professionally. The messy family dynamics. The unconventional path. The time you failed spectacularly.

Now here's the thing: I'm not suggesting you share this in your next team retreat. Corporate environments still have rules about what's "appropriate," and when you're starting a business, some stories feel too risky to lead with. But this story is your secret weapon.

Once you've written it down, let it percolate. Don't analyze it to death or force connections. Instead, gently ask yourself, How does this experience show up in my work life? When do I recognize similar patterns with my team or clients? What do I understand about leadership, about people, about resilience, because of what I've been through?

Trust that the insights will come.

Sometimes it's immediate—"Oh, that's why I'm so good at managing conflict." Sometimes it takes days or weeks for the connection to surface. Be patient with the process.

It's what makes you understand your team's (or your clients') hidden struggles. It's why you can read between the lines when someone says they're "fine." It's your ability to connect with the human behind the crusty professional mask.

This story doesn't need to be edited into your LinkedIn bio. It needs to inform your work. The emotional intelligence you developed from your challenges is your hard-won expertise.

And then very simply, start practicing boundaries. Just say no. For small things you would normally say yes to, say no. This is just practice, so there's no getting it wrong.

Here's why this matters: Every "no" creates space. Space to think and feel and to allow new insights to emerge. When you're constantly saying yes to everyone else's agenda, there's no room left for *your* wisdom to surface. But when you create that space, even in small ways, you give yourself the freedom to access a new level of clarity and power.

The courage it takes to say no to the small stuff is the same energy you'll need to trust your story, your experiences, and to show up as an authentic leader.

It's all connected.

Because choosing yourself professionally starts with choosing yourself personally. Your liberation isn't about oversharing; it's about no longer apologizing for the wisdom your experiences gave you.

CHAPTER THREE

Don't Ask So Many Questions:

How Unearthing Memories Helps You Face (and Manage) the Bitterest Truths

By 11:00 p.m., my tentmates were helping me pack my trunk in a hurry. In three hours, I'd be home. In three days, my father would be gone. But right then, I was still a kid at summer camp who didn't know how the story ended.

Rick, my cousin's husband, was loading it all into the back of his car after Closing Campfire. We didn't speak for the entire drive back home to Westchester. My father was dying. Or maybe he already had.

The summer of 1984 was supposed to be like any other—swimming, arts and crafts, friendship bracelets. Instead, it became the flashpoint that divided my life into before and after. That was the year my father was sick and I was sent to sleepaway camp in Huntington, Massachusetts. Not to escape, but to protect me from watching him fade away, and to give me one last summer that felt like a childhood.

Camp Norwich sat at the end of a wide dirt road, tucked into the foothills of the Berkshires.

Being there gave me a strange and comforting kind of peace, not because I forgot what was happening at home, but because I didn't have to carry it every day. This was my first lesson in how love worked in my family—by creating distance between you and the things that might break you.

There was only one glimpse, one crack in the spell, and it came on Visitors Day.

When my father stepped out of our late 1970s lemon-yellow two-door Chevette, I barely recognized him. His pants hung off his body so baggy, they belonged to a bigger, more vibrant version of him. His cheekbones stuck out sharp and hollow where his warm chubby smile used to be. Even his teeth looked different, as if they didn't fit right in his mouth anymore, protruding outward, their shape so distracting.

He looked as if he were disappearing. Every summer before, I remember running up into his arms and him catching me. His frame so sturdy and strong I never in a million years thought I could knock him over. But this time, instead of the run and jump, I hugged him gently.

His soft white cotton V-neck, which used to fit tight around his stocky frame, hung loose. His jeans, bunched at the waist, were held up by the black leather belt he used to threaten us with, a belt he never needed before. Now it was the only thing holding him together.

He didn't smell like my dad. He smelled like chemo mixed with his quickly decaying body. It wasn't him anymore; it was him *and* cancer that came to visit me that day. But I plastered on a fake smile as long as I could until it physically hurt, and for the whole visit I acted as though nothing was different.

He was dying. And not talking about it didn't make it any less true.

I knew then that something was really wrong. Not just because of how he looked, but because of how everyone else looked at him, as if we were already practicing how to remember him.

I spent the next two weeks trying to forget what I'd seen that day, but I couldn't shake the image of him disappearing before my eyes. I went through the motions of camp life, but part of me was already gone. That's when my family decided it was time—I left for home just after Closing Campfire, a ritual where all six camp units gathered with the counselors and camp staff to sing songs old and new, one last chorus of inside jokes and smoky goodbyes before our parents came to pick us up the next day.

Everyone else was holding the month's memories, promising one another that they'd be back the next year and would stay in touch. I was just trying to make it through the night. Because every morning for four weeks, I had woken up wondering if my father was still alive.

Sending me there was an act of love. Love and denial. How often they come tangled together in Latino families. They sent me away to spare me from death, but in doing so, they taught me that some things are too heavy to witness and too painful to speak.

When I finally returned home, the house had changed, and the inevitability of his death became the lens through which I saw everything.

The Beautiful Burden

The house had gone into full death mode, and yet, strangely, it was one of the most beautiful chapters of my childhood.

Not because of what was happening. But because of who was

there. My father's sisters had arrived. Ida, Nora, and a handful of my cousins. They weren't the side of the family I grew up around and their presence felt different. Comforting.

There was no drama in the air. No nervous hovering. Just warmth, singing, and the pungent smell of fresh culantro, ajo, and comino drifting through the house—that promise of cocina criolla that could heal our broken hearts but couldn't heal my dad.

They moved as if they'd done this before, joyfully chopping, stirring, and dancing around the kitchen elevating the mood. My titi Ida was a pastor's wife, which is why I figured she was so good at loving us all through this crisis.

And the singing, there was so much singing at home and also in his hospital room—my father joining in with his spontaneous harmonizing whenever he had the strength. Of course he loved this. The music and joy in their voices, trying to lift us above all the sadness, was everything he'd grown up with. It was what he tried to re-create at home with his record player, weekend symphonies, and those impromptu vocal arrangements that turned our kitchen into a concert hall. Music held my father's family together and he used it to hold us together too.

But these beautiful moments would fracture when some well-meaning family friend would kneel down and grab my hand and lock eyes with me and say something like "You've gotta be strong for your mom now, okay?"

It wasn't a question or a suggestion. These words lived in their mouths like a programmed reflex, waiting for times exactly like this to ruin a perfectly sane moment.

I don't remember the first time someone said it. I just remember how often.

And how quickly it became the job I didn't know I had applied for. Hold space for her, stay strong for her, and disappear a little.

"Be strong for your mother."

"She needs you right now."

"You're such a good daughter."

You hear something enough times, you start to think you chose it. But I didn't. It was installed. And sometimes, it's embedded so tenderly in kitchens filled with song, in houses that smell like sofrito, mixed with love and memories, that we ignore how heavy it feels to bear.

Until years later, when our bodies still don't know how to relax. Because no one ever told us the job was over.

That's the thing about handed-down beliefs. There's no orientation for this. No one sits us down and explains what's happening and what comes next. We unconsciously absorb them the way humidity in the air gently lays itself on our skin. Like dust particles that can only be seen when a sunbeam shines into a space just right, they float all around us and land wherever they choose, background music that feels like the soundtrack of your life that you didn't realize was playing.

The Love That Doesn't Speak

When withholding is mistaken for love, it shows up in carefully coded language like "She doesn't need to know that." Or "Let's not worry her." Or "Don't say anything in front of the kids."

The intention is love but the impact is conditioning. And over time, it feels more like a reflex and a whole way of being that you never question. The warning so subtle we have no idea we're even being taught.

Years later, during an interview we were doing for the film, my childhood friend shared a memory I had completely forgotten. Or maybe I had been told, but had learned to tune it out so completely it felt like it never happened.

Brothers from Another Mother

I can't think about my childhood without also thinking about Augie and Omar. Our parents were friends before any of us existed. Their mom was a single mother and at the time my mom's closest friend. We practically grew up together. Church on Sundays, Jones Beach trips and camping adventures every summer, and our place or theirs for most holidays and countless weekends.

For years, we made the hour drive to attend church services with them. The entire worship was in Spanish, and their version of Sunday school was brutal. So we made a habit of sneaking out to explore. Discovery missions included poking through closets, nosing through paperwork in open file cabinets in rooms we weren't supposed to be in, going outside and playing on the well-worn fire escape, and eventually ending up in the dusty courtyard of the basement floor, which is where we decided to film this scene for the documentary.

We sat together, Omar, Augie, Gogi (my oldest brother), and me, in the same space where we'd avoided rules and boredom in equal measure. The interview lasted over two hours, and I kept going in and out of "directing mode" because the pull to be a sister was much stronger. Eventually, we ended up sitting there together, remembering.

At one point, Omar leaned forward, curious. "Do you remember that Christmas? My mom told us not to say anything. She didn't want us to bring it up."

"Bring what up?" I said.

"When there weren't a lot of presents under the tree? Remember?"

I blinked. "What?"

I had zero memory of a Christmas without presents. But apparently, my parents were struggling financially, and before the trio left the Bronx for our house, their mom, Loida, pulled them aside and told them not to mention it.

My parents didn't owe me full disclosure. I understand now that kids don't need to carry everything. But still, something about learning this so many years later, from someone else, left me spinning.

Why didn't I know?

I wondered if I had heard it before but tuned it out because my body had already learned these things were not mine to know.

I share this story not to blame my parents but to give language to something deeper.

The instinct to protect is often handed down as love. But over time, that withholding becomes an entire worldview, a lens we start seeing everything through, especially ourselves.

The Language of Secrets

Spanish was the language of secrets in our house. The one my parents used when something felt too big for us to hear. They rarely left the room to talk and didn't wait until we were asleep to discuss sensitive things. They just switched languages. And we all stayed in the room, present and excluded.

The shift in frequency was instant. Their words came out faster and easier. This was their first language, their home, and I could feel the comfort of it. Their bubble expanded, filling the center of the room, while I stayed put on the periphery.

My body knew the drill before my brain caught up. I didn't leave the room; I didn't have to. I evaporated. I tried so hard to dissolve into the background. It's like when you're reading on your phone and someone's talking to you; you're there but you're not really there. Except I didn't need a screen to disappear.

I understood every word; that was the problem. When I heard "No podemos pagar . . ." or "¿Qué vamos a hacer?" floating across the living room, I wanted to ask questions. But questions about grown-up conversations weren't welcome. So I listened without hearing, the way you can sing along to a song for years without really processing what the lyrics mean.

There were three levels to this method I'd developed. Level one was tune out completely, let their voices become background noise. Level two was pay attention but don't get curious. Level three was understand fully, but by then they'd usually notice my attention and leave the room.

And eventually, I began to tune them out because I could tell, by the shift in their tone, that I wasn't invited. The harder the conversations got, the more agitated my father's voice became and the easier it was to turn something off inside myself.

That reflex to withdraw myself in the presence of hard truth became a terrible habit. One that haunted me well into adulthood and showed up in the most unexpected places. Avoiding bank statements, dodging difficult conversations, not being able to tolerate when things got too real. Even now, my first instinct is to look away from hard truths, as if my body still remembers that this isn't meant for me to understand.

It's also why I still struggle with Spanish. My brain decided that tuning it out was the only way to stay close without crossing the very perceptible invisible line. We were always allowed to listen. But we weren't allowed to understand, so no clarifying questions allowed, only respectful distance.

Growing up in a bilingual household helped me see that some things don't translate: not just words, but also rules and loyalties. In our house, certain kinds of curiosity were treated like betrayal. And the rules around that were so complex it felt like I needed a cheat sheet for every scenario, so eventually I stopped asking.

I became the girl who could tune out while seeming tuned in. Who learned to take up less space and who could disappear while still sitting at the table with careful listening and some well-timed nods.

But the real distance I needed to create wasn't geographical; it was internal. I had to move away so I could breathe again, so I could ground myself somewhere else. The long shadow of all that trauma—the iron frying pan, my father's death, the pain and sadness that filled our house—had stretched so far that I couldn't hear my own voice anymore. There was endless noise, such heaviness; I couldn't distinguish between what I wanted and what I needed to get away from. All the pain collapsed together.

For decades, I was completely out of touch with myself. I couldn't tell you how I really felt about anything. There was just how I knew I should feel.

I *should* be married by now.

I *should* have a house.

I *should* call my mom every Sunday.

The list was eternal, and I felt smothered by all of it.

Having learned to disappear myself for so long, I was starving for validation and desperate to be saved. I started seeking relationships where I could disappear into the hopes and dreams of whichever man I was with, never thinking twice about my own value or what I wanted. It wasn't until my mid-thirties, after a devastating breakup where my boyfriend told me, "I love you but I'm not in love with you," that something finally snapped into place.

After we broke up, I had what I can only describe as a "hell no" moment. I decided I would only date someone who was actually right for me from now on. I made a list, and this man better show up exactly as written, no compromises, no settling. It was either that or stay single forever, and suddenly, for the first time in my life, I was okay with being alone.

That resolute decision wasn't the first time I listened to my own voice. I'd been hearing it calling me for years, but it was muffled and distorted beneath the weight of desperation and old wounds. Because I was so disconnected from myself, it became easy to dismiss those internal nudges as inconvenient. I rarely acted in my best interest in relationships. I was, simply put, starving for love, for reassurance, for all the things that had been withheld from me. My heart carried a slow-burning longing, and I thought it was because I didn't have a man. I didn't register the ache was the feeling of abandoning myself. (I did eventually meet and marry a wonderful man, Kevin, but that's another story!)

I'd heard my voice before, but this time I didn't dismiss it. It was the first time I recognized it as the deepest kind of wisdom I possessed. When my truth comes now, the hairs on my forearms stand up. When it's something really true, my thighs get chills. I used to need elaborate pros-and-cons lists to make any significant decision because my intuition was buried so deep. Now I let my body lead.

This is how I learned to distinguish between the inherited voices in my head and my own voice. My truth comes in feelings, in certainty beyond certainty. And I have a rule now: If I don't know what to do, it's always a no.

But this awakening didn't happen overnight. For years, I believed the only way to survive my family's patterns was to run from them entirely. Distance felt like victory—the farther I got from home, the more separate I felt. But I was still tethered to those expectations, still making decisions based on invisible strings that stretched across any distance.

At the time, I thought that was the only way to win the game. Run far enough, and maybe the rules wouldn't follow.

This avoidance pattern followed me into my financial life in ways I'm only now understanding.

When my ex-fiancé was in law school, I automatically became the financial backbone without our ever discussing it. I supported us both, using credit cards because asking him to contribute felt selfish; he was "investing in our future," right? I covered rent, groceries, car insurance on two cars, convinced I could pay it back with the next paycheck. Head fully in the sand in my twenties, I never mapped out what three years of this would actually cost or what would happen if something went wrong. When I was unexpectedly laid off, I found myself holding all the debt when we broke up, and instead of asking him to cover half of what we'd accumulated together, I absorbed it all. The same pattern reasserted itself: overgiving, underasking, avoiding the difficult conversations that might have kept things fair.

For decades, money represented something deeper than currency to me; it was peace, stability, the calm I'd been deprived of amid all the chaos. My father's unpredictable temper, his untimely death, the bullying I endured at school—I'd grown up knowing my mother loved me, but drowning in drama. I externalized the source of that peace, waiting for someone else to handle the hard parts, the same way I'd learned to hold my breath in the room when adult conversations switched to Spanish, only relaxing when they returned to English and I could breathe again.

But there was another layer I overlooked, the cultural bind that made financial success feel like selling out. In my family, there was often talk about "rich people" as fundamentally different from us. We weren't poor, but "rich" was criticized, othered. This created what we call *ni de aquí, ni de allá*—"not from here, not from there"—a split identity around money where family voices advised, "Don't be greedy, don't forget where you came from," while professional spaces demanded, "Ask for more, build wealth, invest."

That cultural dissonance creates an inner tug-of-war that I now recognize in so many of my clients. One foot on the gas, one foot on the brake. Talented, ambitious Latinas unconsciously sabotage their momentum because financial stability feels like betraying one side of their identity.

Sound familiar? Those money patterns are rarely about lack of intelligence. They are about unresolved patterns being replayed in our financial lives.

That cycle cost me in real money and security. It's embarrassing to admit. How could this happen to someone earning five figures for an hour onstage? Because I was constantly at war with myself. Part of me was this confident professional who could command a room, and part of me was still that girl who learned not to ask for too much. I never learned how to let them coexist.

What happened next wasn't because of these cultural patterns or poor financial planning. What happened was completely outside my control. But when the crisis hit, all those old family patterns kicked in and made everything so much harder to navigate.

The wake-up call came like a punch to the gut. When my DEI speaking work dried up because of the political climate, I'd already lost $75,000 in revenue. One cancellation I could handle, maybe two. But by the fourth, fifth, sixth cancellation, I was sitting at my kitchen table with a calculator, watching our life unravel in real time. The bills for my daughter's dance classes? Unpaid. The rent? Late. Credit cards? Maxed out and mounting. I remember the exact moment it crystallized. Our entire financial life was more precarious than I'd ever admitted to myself. It almost had to happen this way—this catastrophically—because if it had not, there was always another gig around the corner, another excuse to avoid facing the truth.

I couldn't sleep at night, worried that we'd end up having to sleep in the car or move into my friend's basement. I kept telling myself I was overreacting, but the numbers didn't lie. We were that close.

Pause and Reflect

Before we go any further, I want you to stop here. If you're facing your own crisis—financial, professional, or personal—this is where the real work begins. Take a minute to answer these questions to help you get grounded in the truth because, trust me, I know how easy it is to believe everything is falling apart.

1. What parts of this mess are out of your control?
2. What do people actually say about your work (not what you think they say)? Write their exact words here (Tip: I have a folder in my phone with screenshots of every nice thing anyone has ever said about me and my

work; if you don't have something like this, create it now so you can have a place to go to remind you of the truth.)

3. Make a list of the places where you still feel powerful. (Maybe it's when you're walking, making your bed, maybe it's that one workout you love, or volunteering your time helping out a friend or neighbor.) Whatever it is, go do that thing right now. Your brain doesn't know the difference—the feeling of power in one area can remind you who you are everywhere else.

You can't prepare for your entire industry becoming politically toxic overnight. But instead of recognizing that external reality, I went straight into self-blame mode. I went into action immediately—I tried every strategy that had worked before, reached out to every contact, pivoted in every direction I could think of. But nothing stuck. It was like drowning when I knew how to swim, but my arms weren't working. All my best ideas failed miserably. Whenever I'd needed to generate more business in the past, I knew exactly what to do. I beat myself up for not having more of a cushion, for not being smarter, for not seeing it coming, when the truth was, I was fighting a battle I couldn't win with weapons that no longer worked.

This required an identity shift of the highest magnitude.

Avoiding the truth was no longer more comfortable than facing it, and that shift told me something fundamental had changed in me. I'd reached the bottom of the next level of my life, and there was something oddly comforting about that recognition. At least I was progressing to the next level.

Now I'm in foreign territory. I'm a professional beginner again, remembering that I am the source—not in a harsh "no one's coming to save you" way, but in an empowering "you have more agency than you ever realized" way.

I model self-compassion now because I don't want to pass down self-flagellation to my daughters. They need to see me being kind and patient with myself, especially when I'm learning something new at fifty-five. My story isn't over, and I want them to witness compassionate triumph so that when life gets tough for them, they know something more is possible.

My first major financial mistake was also my most expensive lesson in boundaries I didn't know I was allowed to set.

Back then, I stepped into the financial role without hesitation. Not because we discussed it or planned for it, but because that's what felt natural to me. The overgiving, underasking pattern I'd learned at home kicked in without question.

I took on more than I could reasonably manage. And when my salary wasn't enough, I put things on credit cards, convinced it would all work out somehow. I never asked him to contribute his student loan money.

When we broke up, I was left holding all the debt. I didn't understand interest rates, how they compounded, or that this debt would follow me for many years. Women had only been allowed to get credit cards without a male cosigner since 1974. I was born in 1970, so financial independence was brand-new. My mother's generation was still learning too, which meant there was zero wisdom to pass down about what financial partnership should look like.

The only rule she gave me was "Don't get into debt."

I took on all the financial burden, blaming myself for being too generous. I couldn't even see that accountability was an option.

The Survival Mentality

It never hit me like a lightning bolt, that *Oh my God, I don't know anything about money.* I just assumed I had to figure everything out on my own. That was my normal.

Fight or flight convinces you that functioning is enough. And if you're not actively drowning, you must be fine.

And when you live in that state long enough, you stop even looking for the shore.

Gabor Maté talks about how trauma doesn't just take the form of flashbacks or panic attacks, it shows up as disconnection from self. For me, that disconnection showed up financially. I made good money, but emotionally I still felt that I was barely scraping by. I couldn't access a sense of security, even when the numbers suggested I should feel safe.

That was the first clue that something deeper was going on. My body was still living in the past, even when my circumstances had changed.

It wasn't until I moved to Denver that the fog started to lift. A mutual friend introduced me to a woman in finance, a successful single mom who owned a beautiful home in Castle Rock. I asked how she'd built so much on her own.

She told me about her upbringing, which was far more traumatic than mine, and then she said something that gave me pause.

"I taught myself everything. Finance, real estate, investing, I studied it all. No one saved me. I built everything I have from nothing."

Her story mirrored mine in many ways, but the outcomes were radically different. And for the first time, I understood that it wasn't just about trauma. It was about what you do after. She didn't wait for a green light. She learned the system that was never designed for us and used it.

That moment rattled me because I'd always assumed self-reliance meant I had to figure it out as I went. But what I'd really been doing was coping, not building.

I started to see the holes in my financial foundation:

I didn't know how mortgages worked.

I didn't understand credit utilization.

No one had ever explained compound interest, the stock market, or even why your first home is rarely your dream home, but instead a stepping stone.

We could've purchased a starter condo back when my husband, Kevin, and I were engaged, but I turned it down because it wasn't "perfect," and neither of us understood that it wasn't supposed to be. No one told me the goal was equity, not aesthetics.

That one decision still haunts me not because of the money we lost, but because it revealed how much I didn't know. But regret is expensive, and I try not to live there anymore. Instead, I use it to inform the decisions I make today.

Learning to Trust the Future

The real challenge wasn't understanding money, it was trusting I could have a future at all. Trauma teaches you to focus on now. Not five years from now. Not retirement. Just right now. The shift from a stress-response mode to long-term thinking required an emotional rewiring.

Even after reading countless financial books and binging YouTube videos, the hardest part was facing the emotional resistance and my reflex to shut down, check out, or minimize my needs.

Especially in my marriage. Talking about money with clients is so much easier than talking about money with my husband. It's still hard because sometimes when things get heavy, when I don't have answers or I feel like a complete idiot for making some of the decisions we made, I get so tired I literally can't keep my eyes open. This response is so deeply ingrained into my nervous system that my physiology tries to shut down the conversation before it even begins.

So, we got strategic. We started scheduling money conversations in advance, putting them on the calendar like real business meetings:

"Tuesday at noon. Let's talk about the budget."

It gave me structure. It made the conversation feel less personal and more doable.

We'd listen to financial podcasts together and pause to discuss. I'd notice the old feelings surface—guilt, defensiveness, fear—and try not to let them drive the conversation.

Because I want something different. Because we both do. And the only way anything changes in a relationship is if both people are willing to change themselves.

Breaking the Cycle

We make it a point to talk about money in front of our kids. Always. We don't censor it or sugarcoat it. That alone makes our home radically different from the one I grew up in.

I never overheard a single real conversation (in English) about money as a child. The only time it came up was in this funny, ritualistic way. I'd ask my dad, "What would you do if we won the lottery?" And every single time, he'd say, "Pay bills."

That was the tone around money in our house: tense, stretched thin, and slightly tragic. Money wasn't something you planned with or got curious about. It was something you survived and something you hoped would finally stop being a problem, but never actually talked about.

In my home, it sounds different. Money is part of life, like ice cream or weekend plans, not something heavy or shameful. We talk about it openly, casually, and without energetic weight.

When I discovered the credit card points game after years of work travel, I got obsessed. I was late to the party and could've accumulated so many more points had I started earlier, but once I understood the system, I wanted to master it.

And I brought the girls into the process with me.

Every time our credit score went up, they knew. They saw what impacted it—e.g., on-time payments, debt ratios, card limits—and learned how each action affected our financial future. When we finally qualified for premium cards, I explained the difference between cash-back cards, travel points, hotel loyalty programs.

It became fun, not just to learn it, but to teach it.

They now understand credit as a tool, not something to fear. It can be useful if you're responsible and pay off the balance—if you know how to work the system. It's like an extension of my Latino resourcefulness. We've enjoyed airport lounges all over the world because of this strategy.

Beyond credit, we've talked about high-yield savings accounts, investing basics, how mortgages work, and 401(k)s. Do I know everything? Absolutely not. But I've stopped waiting to be an expert before I share what I'm learning. The point isn't perfection; it's normalizing the conversation.

And it's not just the good stuff. They hear us talk about the hard parts too.

They've lived through the abundant years and through the recent struggle. They know what it looks like when we're thriving, and when we need to tighten up. We don't lie. We don't pretend. We don't try to protect them from reality by hiding it.

They know what it means to cook at home more; to pause on planning big vacations; and, unfortunately, to scale back Christmas. Do I love the idea of my kids seeing us struggle financially? Of course not. But I am proud of how we've handled it and we are closer as a family because of it.

They've seen a mom who made a movie with no experience, built a multiple six-figure speaking career, and provided abundantly for them. They've also seen that same mom navigate a tough year when politics shifted and speaking work dried up. They've watched me be scared and still show up, get creative, and hold on to the belief that if I built something once, I have the capacity and the know-how to build it again.

And that might be an even more important lesson than "follow your dreams." They're learning that resilience doesn't mean avoiding hard times. It means trusting yourself through them.

For most of my life, I would contort myself into impossible shapes to sidestep uncomfortable conversations. When we faced financial devastation this past year, every instinct screamed at me to disappear, to hide from the dance studio about unpaid bills, to ghost creditors, to fake prosperity while drowning in debt. But I forced myself into a different approach entirely. I wrote those excruciating emails to the school laying bare our financial wreckage, sharing my fragile optimism about uncertain opportunities, and begging for grace I wasn't sure I deserved. I stripped myself naked financially in front of several businesses, offering transparency as my only currency.

Everything in my DNA told me that revealing the truth would detonate my world. But what I discovered was the complete opposite: People responded with a grace so profound it rewrote my understanding of human nature. It was agony, but I didn't die. And more important, I discovered I am someone I can respect when I choose honesty over deception. Truth, even when it burns, is infinitely easier than the exhausting theater of pretending.

Growing up marinated in family taboos and secrets didn't break me, it forged me. All those years of surviving on crumbs of information, of developing supernatural radar for what was being hidden, of starving for authentic truth, that's what made me masterful at helping other people excavate what they're burying in their own lives.

Now *I* channel that same intuition professionally. I can smell avoidance from across a room because I lived in its suffocating cloud my entire childhood. The very thing that felt like a curse became my most potent gift. And learning to handle my own brutal truths with grace instead of destruction is the transformation I facilitate every single day.

She challenges assumptions and her belief in herself grows.

Reflection and Practice

Pick one of these and either journal about it or grab coffee with someone you trust and do this together.

> **The tune-out pattern:** Think about the last time you mentally checked out during an important conversation, maybe a budget meeting, performance review, or even a difficult family discussion. Were you protecting yourself from being overwhelmed, or were you abandoning your right to understand something that affects your life?

The "I should know this already" shame: What's one area where you carry secret shame about what you don't know? Money? Corporate politics? Family history? What would be possible if you gave yourself permission to be a beginner at something important?

Your family's unspoken rules: What's one thing your family never directly told you not to ask about, but you learned not to anyway? How is that same "don't ask too many questions" energy showing up in your professional life right now? What micro-action can you do to begin to change it?

CHAPTER FOUR

¡Bájale Dos Rayitas!

How to Defy the Patriarchy to Reclaim Your Divine Beauty and Power

I'm about to tell you something that might make you uncomfortable. Something that goes against everything we've been taught about humility, motherhood, and what it means to be a "good Latina." But I'm starting to think everything we learned about beauty was designed to make us abandon ourselves.

What I'm still learning is that beauty isn't about vanity. It's about divinity. And when I abandon it, I abandon my most holy self.

Divinity to me is that peace-giving act of remembering. Not religious necessarily, but sacred—that place where all possibilities live. It's what I see in babies—pure potential, innocence, and wisdom, all at once. And when I connect with that divine essence in myself, I can recognize it in others too. There's something particularly powerful about our shared culture—that shorthand we have as Latinas, when we don't have to prove ourselves first, when someone just gets it. That recognition, that ability to get each other without explanation—that's our divine cultural connection.

I wasn't always afraid of being seen.

As a little girl, I loved the way my body moved. Gymnastics made me feel strong and capable. I climbed trees, rode bikes, got dirty, ran with the neighborhood boys through the woods behind our house. My body never felt like a limitation, it felt like freedom.

I had wild, curly, bouncy hair and was considered a cute kid.

A photographer stopped my mother on the streets of New York City, asking to take pictures of me for his portfolio. I sat for him twice. She said regular people would stop her in the street just to look at me and tell her how cute I was. When we moved to Westchester, a photographer in our neighborhood asked my mom if I could model for him. And I loved every minute of it. The lights, the direction, the way he'd move me just so to catch the perfect pose. It felt good to be seen, to be chosen, to have someone think I was worth capturing.

But everything shifted when I hit puberty and started developing. Suddenly, my mother's friends would tell her how beautiful I was and how I "looked older than my age." I could see it made her uncomfortable, and it made me feel uneasy too. As if they were trying to make me a woman when I was still just a girl.

That's when the restrictions started. Anything that showed my midriff was a no-no. Tight clothes that emphasized my body, absolutely not. Shirts that were too revealing, jeans that were too fitted, don't even think about it. Beauty had become something that needed to be managed, monitored, and contained.

The little girl who loved being photographed was learning new rules. And I carried those rules with me for decades, until this past summer when everything changed.

This past summer, at my absolute lowest point, I was walking through my neighborhood when a red-throated hummingbird appeared out of nowhere right in front of me. Weightless but like she was carrying a message. Then a squirrel scurried past with a nut in its mouth, and a dog walker that I recognized smiled as she walked past me. Everything was alive and enough and exactly as it should be. It was so damn obvious it hurt. I'd been listening to my coaching clients this way for years, seeing my friends this way, recognizing the sacred in everyone except myself.

If all of it was worthy, then so was I.

When this revelation clicked for me—worthiness over vanity—I realized I'd been hemorrhaging my power for decades, chasing external validation like a drug I could never quite get enough of. Here's the thing, though: When you believe you're not enough, you're chasing something that doesn't exist. "Enough" isn't measurable. It's not calculable. It's a mathematical impossibility. You can't accumulate sufficient accomplishments, shed sufficient pounds, or check off sufficient boxes to achieve permanent enoughness. I'd inhabited a great shape before, draped myself in beautiful clothes, and even then I dissected myself mercilessly—convinced I could be thinner, smoother, more flawless somehow. The goalpost was ever moving and evaporated the moment I got close to it because I was scavenging for worth outside myself instead of recognizing the inherent power pulsing through my own flesh.

Not until I began treating my body as something precious, believing that my skin and bones and battle scars were enough, did everything shift. Instead of conducting forensic examinations of my flaws, I revolutionized my entire relationship with beauty. I started seeing myself as something holy. And when you believe in your own holiness, your own divinity, kindness to yourself stops feeling scarce and like something you have to earn or dole out in careful portions and becomes something that flows freely, abundantly.

This is how we fight back: not with anger, but with love for ourselves.

Here's the question that exploded my old worldview: Who profits from your belief that you're inadequate? Because it's sure as hell not you. In the "enoughness" economy, we're perpetual debtors with no agency and no authority. But when we start honoring ourselves as divine, we reclaim our power. And that terrifies every system designed to keep us kneeling.

That morning on my walk, I repeated a new mantra to myself: *I'm brilliant. I'm fabulous. I'm fucking magnetic.* And something changed in how I was finally seeing myself.

I used to think reclaiming beauty meant going back to some earlier version of me. A thinner me, a younger version. The one who was up for anything that sounded like an adventure.

But what I'm discovering in the sweat of my morning walks, in the small, ordinary moments when I choose to actually care, is that this is about staying awake and about refusing to fall into the *trance of helplessness.* That seductive, familiar state where we convince ourselves we have no choices.

It's wild how fast we'll sacrifice our own truth to keep everyone else comfortable. How we learn that our self-denial is more valuable than our healing.

Fuck that trance.

This chapter is about claiming our divine beauty now. Like right now. In the middle of some of the hardest chapters of my life. Because I'm not letting myself down again. I'm worth staying present for, and so are you.

And more than that, I'm still here. Still discovering how good it can really get.

Where It Started

This story doesn't begin with a mirror or a makeover. It starts with the women who came before me and the impossible standards they carried like gospel.

I'm fifteen, getting ready for church, and my mom's eyes do that thing—the scan. Up and down. Pausing at my chest, my hips. "Ese vestido es muy tight," she says, shaking her head. Too tight. Too much. I change into something shapeless, something safe, and watch myself fade in the mirror. That scan taught me to see myself through the eyes of judgment first, beauty second. I learned to disappear myself before anyone else could do it for me.

Because being too attractive was wrong, and being wholesome was right. Being skinny was good and being chubby was sloppy and not good. And there was this sliver of danger around being ever so plump where my boobs and butt seemed voluptuous and sexy. And that was very, *very* bad.

The math was impossible: Use your assets but don't be too attractive. Too visible meant you were "asking for it." Too invisible meant you were wasting it. The space between them was razor-thin, and no one ever taught any of us how to navigate it. If you too grew up with impossible beauty standards, you know what it feels like to be told you're too much and not enough at the same time, and that this game feels as if it were rigged from the start.

DENISE SOLER COX

Ana's "Dangerous" White Bikini

When I think about beauty, I don't feel light or free. I feel watched and I still sometimes feel afraid.

My cousin Gloria had my favorite house in Puerto Rico. Lots of land, a pool, a wrought-iron gate. Lush Caribbean countryside grew over and through the steel that protected the property from every angle. Her home always felt modern. Freer. Gloria was sharp, educated, forward-thinking, and bikinis weren't a big deal in her house. But her mother, and my mother, and our aunts carried generations of unspoken limits that day, their disapproving glances speaking volumes in the language of las tías.

The physical gates were outside. The cultural ones stayed inside. These weren't just rules the tías were upholding with their chisme. They were taboos, immutable and uncrossable lines.

A familiar hush fell over the kitchen when I walked in. The hairs on my neck stood up. It meant someone was being talked about, and usually, when it came to these three, that someone was me. But this time, thankfully, I wasn't the target.

Their gossip was so hypnotic I wanted to be part of it. After all, I wasn't the one they were dissecting.

I strained to hear them say a name, trying to look casual as I leaned in closer. Watched where their puckered lips pointed, their bobbing chins, the way their eyes widened, brows pulled up as high as they could go, as if they'd just been surprised, directing your gaze without ever lifting a finger. That unmistakable Puerto Rican body language.

They were gesturing to the pool.

I stepped into a beam of Puerto Rican summer sunlight spilling through the window to get a look at whom they were talking about.

The yard was a burst of heat and sound. "Suavemente" by Elvis Crespo blasted from the speaker near the pool. Everyone knew the words. The melody was contagious, joyfully Puerto Rican. That song always meant someone was having a party.

And there she was.

Ana. My second cousin. Radiant and utterly magnetic in that white bikini. She looked absolutely incredible.

Even before I had the language for it, something in me understood this was my first glimpse of the cost of female power. Ana wasn't doing anything wrong; she was just being her fabulous self. But her joy threatened people who had abandoned their own, so they needed to snuff out hers.

This is what generational shame looks like. It limits you and makes you resent anyone who dares live the life you convinced yourself you couldn't have.

I wasn't even the one wearing it, but something inside me felt guilty, as if Ana's bikini was a problem waiting to happen.

"Ella parece easy," my titi Carmen said, taking an audible sip of her freshly prepared café con leche.

They all nodded in agreement. My mom, her sister, even Ana's grandmother, bonding over their shared disapproval.

I couldn't stop watching Ana.

Did she know what they were saying? How could she? We were inside in the air-conditioning, and she was out in the pool living her best life. But did she notice how that pervert in the water was looking at her? As if he were peeling off her bikini with his eyes. So nasty. I don't think she noticed. Good for her.

And then it escalated.

A game of chicken began. The tías and I watched aghast from behind the glass sliding doors as the strange man, someone none of us knew, ducked underwater, placed his head between Ana's legs. The water churned around them, turning white with foam, agitated like the waves at Playa Azul on the days we weren't allowed to swim. He pushed up from the bottom with a thrust that masqueraded as fun, hoisting her onto his shoulders in one dramatic motion. Her wet legs draped over his neck, and her bikini bottoms pressed against the bare skin of his neck.

From behind the sliding glass door, we stared into what felt like a fishbowl—the pool area where this violation was playing out. Another cousin climbed onto Ana's brother's shoulders and the game was on.

"Ay, Dios," one of the tías sighed. "Pero no tiene vergüenza." Their forearms lifted, palms out, fingers together. The classic Puerto Rican don't-blame-me gesture.

They clutched their chests as if they were witnessing something obscene. As if Ana's joy were a personal attack on everything they'd spent their lives upholding.

Titi Carmen stormed outside, and I followed. Not out of concern (let's be honest), but out of pure curiosity. I marched behind her like her assistant, carefully placing myself for the perfect view of any and all drama.

Bending over the pool, she said to the man, "Excuse me. My niece needs to come inside right now.

"Ana, your grandmother needs you."

Ana laughed. "Okay."

Light and polite and apologetic as she slid off his shoulders, backward and into the water.

She emerged from the pool radiant and unbothered. A towel wrapped around her now. Her power contained.

She was too young to know what she'd just done, or maybe she did. Maybe some part of her understood this was the cost of beauty? I'm not sure.

That moment has stayed with me for years.

We internalize this contradictory lesson as girls: that our joy, our confidence, our visible happiness, threatens other women. That we're supposed to dim our light so others don't feel bad about dimming theirs. That female power is a zero-sum game where one woman's radiance somehow diminishes everyone else's.

Maybe you have had an Ana moment too, a time when you witnessed another woman's bliss being policed and part of you felt both envious and threatened or something else. That's the moment we learn that our light might be too bright for others to handle.

I was uneasy too. I wasn't just watching Ana. I was watching the version of myself I had been taught to fear. Her bikini wasn't just a swimsuit. It forced me to see everything I didn't yet understand about desire, power, danger, and shame.

In college I had already lived through what radiance could cost. I had already lost my sense of safety. And yet some part of me craved to be my version of her again.

Because even in my fear, I longed for the power I didn't know I'd had before I lost it.

But I had it backward. I hadn't lost my light, I had learned to hide it so well that even I couldn't find it anymore. The real tragedy wasn't that feminine power was dangerous, it was that I had hidden it so thoroughly I didn't know how to get it back.

That's what beauty meant to me for years, longing for a self I didn't know how or if I could reclaim.

Youth Group Retreat

Years before Ana, Tim had taught me that even when I wasn't trying to be noticed, I still wasn't safe. This is how we learn to hide. You're told you're too much, then violated for simply being.

By the time I was in high school, I'd already learned that existing in a female body was a minefield.

It was all unspoken and taught through clothing restrictions and the way women constantly judged other women's bodies under their breath. The impossible binary became obvious: look like a "good girl," wholesome and covered, and never like a "slut," tight and revealing, you get the picture. Though my mother never used the word *slut*, the message lived in her disapproving glances and in every comment about how certain clothes made women look "cheap" or reflected poorly on their character.

I internalized every lesson until they became my own voice. Once my body developed breasts, hips that curved, an actual waist, I began to receive unwanted attention even in the most conservative clothes. This convinced me that if I wore anything more revealing, I'd have an even harder time. That's when I started wondering if certain clothes really did mean I was "asking for trouble."

Despite all these messages, there were moments when I felt powerful in my body. When I was dancing, I felt strong and agile, full of energy and freedom. On the dance floor, I could forget everything else. My hips knew exactly how to move, my arms carved through space like I owned it. I remember this one deep crimson cotton skirt I received as a birthday gift from my aunt. It fit me perfectly, and when I put it on, I felt radiant, like myself. Beautiful, confident and alive.

Dancing in that red skirt, I could imagine what it felt like to live in my body without fear.

But at a youth group retreat I was taught to forget I'd ever been holy at all.

My dad died the August before my freshman year in high school, and church retreats had become a lifeline.

That particular weekend, about ten of us were sleeping in one room with twin beds we'd haphazardly pushed together in a chaotic, messy maze that connected us all. All good kids. The kind of teenagers parents trust on church trips. We stayed up talking until the early hours, then finally fell asleep in that communal space that felt safe by all accounts.

I woke up to heat. Tim's skin wasn't clammy; it was burning, radiating an intense, aggressive warmth. I felt his heavy, hot breath hitting my neck, the rhythm of his long deep pulls of air shivering against my skin.

His hand was completely wrapped around mine, forcing it around him. My own hand felt heavy and disconnected—a dead, limp tool he was manipulating for his pleasure. Around us, the room hummed with the innocent snoring of ten other kids, clueless and safe, while I lay frozen in the dark, my body no longer my own.

I was disgusted. Scared. Embarrassed. Ashamed. And I froze completely.

People talk about what they'd do if something like this happened. Everyone thinks they'd run or fight. But I did neither. My big move was rolling over onto my left side and pulling my hand away, pretending I was still asleep.

That was it.

The next morning, I tried to forget it happened. I didn't tell anyone. He got away with it, and I made him invisible to me from that day forward. That felt like the only power I had, to ice him out completely.

But the damage was done. That night taught me that even when I wasn't trying to be attractive, even when I was literally not conscious,

I still wasn't safe. I started wondering about my clothes, my body, how much space I took up. There seemed to be this force field around me that could draw unwanted attention, one I desperately wanted to learn how to turn off.

The Biggest Price

When I was in college, I found out just how steep the price could be for feeling free and alive. In Allston, Massachusetts, I left a party by myself because the basement was hot as fuck, the floor was sticky, and it just wasn't my jam. The music vibrated against the walls while frat boys in their white togas circled the women as if they were selecting prey. They kept refilling our plastic cups with disgusting red punch, spiked with "tasteless" grain alcohol, from a lined plastic garbage can as if it were some kind of novelty.

At some point, I got separated from my friends. I looked toward the stairs, but it was packed wall to wall with a sweaty, drunken bottleneck of bodies. That's when I spotted an old wooden desk pushed against the wall beneath an open window, and I knew it was my way out.

I remember thinking how ridiculous I must have looked crawling through that window into a dirty alley. But once I was out, I felt relieved. I just needed a minute to catch my breath and figure out how to get back inside to find my friends, who had disappeared in that sea of white fabric and red Solo cups.

That's when he appeared in the window frame.

The same toga-wearing frat boy who'd been watching me all night, whose eyes had followed me in a way that made my skin crawl. When I told him how drunk I was, how everything was spinning, he offered his room to "rest." Said it as if doing me a favor.

My gut screamed danger.

I jumped up and started making my way out of the alley. No map. No cell phone. No goodbye to creepy toga boy. Just this vague memory from campus orientation about using the CITGO sign like some kind of North Star if you ever got lost. I've never been so grateful for a corporate logo in my life.

A few blocks later, I spotted two guys weaving their way down the street. They had also been drinking too much but seemed harmless enough. Safe-ish. The kind of college guys more likely to quote Monty Python than cause me any trouble.

I rushed up to them, my words tumbled out about the party, the creepy toga guy, how I had no idea where I was or how to get back, and did they happen to know which way to the CITGO sign? They were freshmen at Northeastern and just as lost as I was, but we stumbled our way to Comm Ave together, laughing at the things you find silly when you're relieved to be safe. I remember thinking how lucky I'd gotten from sitting alone in that dirty alley to finding my goofy guardian angels.

West Campus

The fluorescent lights of the residence hall lobby felt harsh after coming in from the dark streets. My shoes squeaked against the freshly waxed floor as I walked past security, flashed my ID, and made my way up to the elevator, still riding the wave of my lucky escape.

My side of the floor was eerily still. Completely empty. I checked every room.

Everyone's still at the party, I thought. They were probably wondering where I'd disappeared to. The only signs of life came from the guys' side, where the engineering students lived. The über-nerdy boys I'd also labeled as harmless in my head.

After scouting out my floor and realizing I was the only one home, I drifted past the elevator toward Chris's room. He'd appointed himself my unofficial welcome committee when I moved in a few weeks earlier. The framed photo of his girlfriend back home in Milwaukee prominently displayed on his desk was part of the reason I trusted him.

Inside, I found him drinking with a few guys from the floor. No togas. Just half-empty Budweiser cans and a bunch of boys pretending to be men.

"Have you seen anyone from my side?"

No one had.

"You're the first one back."

I lingered for a few seconds, then told them I wasn't feeling great. Said I'd never drink that disgusting punch again.

I tried to steady my breathing as I walked back to my room past the common area, filled with basic furniture we never sat in. Everything felt tilted, as if the whole building were leaning slightly to the left. I began to feel that I was going to be sick. My key scraped against the lock a few times before I got it right.

I heard the hum of our small refrigerator, rented by the month, keeping snacks and drinks cool and ready for when we wanted them, and I collapsed onto my unmade bed, still in my going-out clothes.

The ceiling spun above me as my eyes got heavy.

And I guess I forgot to lock the door.

The next thing I remember was weight. A heavy, warm blanket pressing me down. My body knew something was very wrong before my brain did. Still swimming in grain alcohol, my mind reached for a safe memory: David.

This felt like the roughhousing of our childhood. I was disoriented. Was I home? Was I dreaming? David was dead, my mind remembered, so this had to be a dream.

But then the smell hit me. Not the grass and sweat of our backyard or the goofy cologne he'd wear for fun. I smelled stale beer. Sharp and sour and gross. And the weight wasn't playful; it was suffocating. I squirmed left and right, trying to get leverage, trying to breathe and get out from under him, but he was smothering me. When I realized I couldn't move, my body went limp and I surrendered the way I did when I wrestled with David—except we'd be laughing, rolling around and having fun. But there was no laughter here. Just the reality of his vile breath on my face.

Chris was on top of me. Inside me.

The alcohol spun my thoughts into mishmash.

I was so close to puking that I convinced myself I was having a nightmare.

If I could just wait it out, he'd disappear, and I'd wake up for real.

Except I was already awake.

And this was already real.

I tried to push him off. Not strong enough. Way too drunk.

Tried again. Still nothing.

The third time, I clawed at his face and tried to scream. But the "No" came out distorted, like when you're numbed at the dentist and your mouth won't shape the sound. That same helpless feeling of waiting for control to return, for your voice to work again.

But this wasn't Novocain wearing off.

This was different.

This was much worse.

I could barely breathe under his weight. Couldn't process what was happening.

Rape.

He was raping me.

My mind kept floating in and out of consciousness, and I remember thinking if I just squeezed my eyes shut tight enough, maybe this would stop. Maybe I could slip back into sleep. Maybe I could float right out of my body and leave it here, until he was done and this was over.

A single warm sunbeam on my face woke me up the next morning.

The room was too bright. Too eerily calm. I was still in my going-out clothes but hadn't yet noticed that I wasn't wearing underwear. My mouth was coated with the sweet-and-sour taste of the nasty red punch from the night before. I looked over and saw that my roommate, Lisa, was back. Thank God. I hadn't known her long, but I adored her, and I was so relieved she was safe.

I couldn't wait to tell her everything.

I stretched and felt . . . wrong. Sore in places that didn't make sense. My body felt different, like it had betrayed some unspoken agreement we'd had.

I shifted and realized I wasn't wearing underwear. The absence felt like evidence I wasn't ready to process.

What haunted me wasn't that my body had failed me; it was that I couldn't control what it seemed to attract. I had trusted my instincts to leave that party, walked those dark Boston streets confidently, and made it home safely. My instincts had worked perfectly.

But then, even in my own room, even asleep, even after doing everything right, it still wasn't enough.

I didn't know how to trust myself when the very intuition that saved me couldn't protect me everywhere. I didn't know how to feel safe in my own body when it felt like a magnet for the wrong kind of attention, no matter what I did.

I started talking to Lisa, the words spilling out. How I'd lost everyone in that sea of freshman partiers. How I'd seen them disappear up the stairs but couldn't reach them through the crowd, so I crawled out that basement window instead. About the creepy toga frat guy following me into the alley, and how I had to get away, which is why my friends never saw me again and I was sorry if I made them worry. About the Northeastern guys, Tim and Adrian, who helped me find my way home, following the CITGO sign like a beacon.

The sun felt warm on my face.

I turned my head toward the window, and that's when I saw it. The Budweiser can sitting on my desk, behind my pillow. Right where he'd left it. Like a fucking receipt. Like proof of what he'd done to me.

And it all came rushing back. Not all at once, but in pieces.

The feeling of him on top of me. The way I couldn't move. How I remembered scratching his face but he still wouldn't stop and how I thought it was a nightmare, but it wasn't.

And my whole body started screaming inside. Not out loud, but in that way only you can hear when your body says:

It happened.

It was real.

It was real.

It was real.

But underneath that scream was another voice, one that sounded suspiciously like my mother's warnings, like every lesson I'd been taught about being careful, about not trusting, about the dangers of being noticed.

This is what happens when you're not careful enough, mija.

The shame hit harder than the memory. I had trusted Chris because he had a girlfriend, that framed photo on his desk was supposed to make him safe. But now I felt as if my judgment had failed me completely. How could I have gotten it so wrong?

Even knowing I'd done nothing wrong, I still felt that somehow my body had made this happen. As if I'd walked right into exactly what I'd been warned about my whole life, and now I'd proven that all those protective rules were necessary after all.

The anger at myself was suffocating. Why hadn't I been more careful? Why had I trusted him?

Why had I forgotten to lock my door?

And underneath it all was the crushing understanding that I was completely alone with this truth. I couldn't tell my mother. She'd turn it into her own grief, my brother's death, her suffering, one more thing piled onto her already unbearable loss. My pain would disappear into hers.

I was trapped between knowing I didn't deserve this and feeling that somehow I'd brought it on myself anyway.

And with those memories came a new belief that would shape everything: If I hadn't been so visible at that party, if I hadn't been noticed, if I had just stayed hidden, this wouldn't have happened. Staying small felt like the only way to stay safe.

But just hours before, I had felt so alive in my body. Dancing in denim shorts and a cotton long-sleeve button-up I'd bought in Spain the summer before, an outfit that made me feel alive and confident. I was having the time of my life, laughing with new friends, getting attention that felt good and fun and validating in all the right ways.

I was at the very beginning of this new version of me, free from all the drama at home, full of hope and possibility. For maybe the first time in my life, I was taking up space without apology.

The attention from guys felt exciting, not dangerous. Just silly, frat-boyish fun that made me feel attractive and alive.

I had been so happy to finally turn the page, to become who I was meant to be.

And now, in one night, all of that ease in my own body, that freedom to be seen and celebrated, felt like a memory from someone else's life. Being visible no longer felt safe and I was changed forever.

Lisa listened. I told her everything, the words spilling out between sobs I couldn't control. She held my hand while I cried.

"Maybe you should tell someone," she said softly.

I knew I wouldn't.

I made her promise not to say a word. Made her swear to keep my secret, even though I could see in her eyes how much it hurt her to agree.

Because if I told, I'd probably have to leave school. And I couldn't leave. Not then. Not after what it took to get there.

But something deeper than logistics was stopping me from telling. I had learned that being seen, being the girl at the party, being noticed, being visible, was dangerous. The solution felt obvious: disappear. Make myself so unnoticeable that nothing like this could ever again happen.

There's a special kind of taboo around speaking these details. As if saying it out loud wouldn't just make it more real, it would mark me. At school. In my family. Forever.

We're taught that our truth is too heavy, too messy, too inconvenient, for the people we love. That speaking up means adding more pain to already-struggling families. That keeping it buried isn't just about protecting the perpetrator, it's about protecting our mothers from one more thing to carry and our families from yet another crisis to navigate. We learn that our healing is less important than everyone else's peace. And with this awareness our light starts to fade. Our belleza becomes a shadow, to outsiders and to ourselves.

Living in Boston by myself, even for just a few weeks, had given me a taste of freedom. The kind I'd been craving for years. And not even being sexually assaulted was going to get in the way of that. So, I stayed. I got silent. And I kept going. Dimmer but more determined, to work, to shove it down, to get things done, to make it all not matter.

Because that's what we do. We persist.

I convinced myself that hiding was smart. If no one could see me, no one could hurt me. Hiding became my way of staying safe.

The unspoken does have a weight though. And it can be carried for years. Sometimes we pack it away so carefully that we forget it's there and we can almost convince ourselves that none of it ever happened.

But your body knows, it always remembers.

And mine was about to remind me.

CHAPTER FIVE

No Se Puede Tapar el Sol con un Dedo: Healing from Trauma and Discovering the Divine Self

I thought I moved to Denver for a fresh start, but the city had been waiting to remind me of a night I spent decades trying to forget.

The Body Really Does Keep Score

A major street cuts through downtown Denver. I learned its name for the first time on a road sign, and my whole body froze. It was his name, or close enough to trigger the memory I'd buried.

Before I moved here, I'd gotten really good at forgetting him and that night.

Not by forcing myself to forget, but by carefully submerging it under the cold depths of my memory, like pushing something deeper and deeper underwater until I couldn't see or feel it anymore, until the surface looked smooth and glassy again. Until I forgot that anything pushed down that deep eventually creates pressure. And pressure always finds a way out.

I came to Denver on a business trip a few months before moving here. Something about the city felt like home. As if it could be my next chapter. I started in Boulder, thinking I'd like the small-town feel mixed with nature. A fresh start in a funky new place. But I outgrew it and moved to Denver a year later.

I found a seven-hundred-square-foot rental inside an old Denver Square near Cheesman Park. It was charming and slightly haunted and perfect.

Except for the constant reminder.

I kept hearing the name. Over and over. Every time I drove. Got directions. Talked to a neighbor.

His name was everywhere.

I didn't expect it to mess with me the way it did.

The name didn't just register in my ears; it hijacked my timeline. Instantly the car dissolved and I was back in the pitch black of my dorm room, helpless and alone. My whole body went tense, like some kind of Pavlovian trauma bell had sounded. Like muscle memory, but for panic.

When I first moved here, my mouth would clamp shut, sealing in a primal scream. A sudden stinging feeling at the skin under my eyes, dragging me down.

I had to force myself to inhale and take a long gulp of oxygen, just to snap myself back into the present. My hands wanted to let go of the wheel and pound the dashboard in pure rage. The sound of his effing name felt like a physical blow that demanded I relive the very thing I'd spent decades trying to lock away.

I tried to ignore it, compartmentalize it. This was my go-to strategy by now. When something felt too big or too scary, I'd retreat into my body, using weight as armor. I'd learned that if I could just hide well enough, maybe the problem would disappear too. But history doesn't disappear just because you ignore it.

We're supposed to "get over it" behind closed doors. To process our pain privately so it doesn't make others uncomfortable. Seeking help means we're defective (instead of brave), and talking about what we've been through makes us feel damaged instead of human.

But the memories kept coming back. Not like one big wave. More like a relentless loop playing in the background of my life.

The toga party.

The CITGO sign.

The emptiness on my side of the floor.

The door left unlocked.

The way I woke up.

The tin beer can on my desk.

And my closing off that followed.

So I booked a session with a hypnotist. Frankly, I thought if I ever paid someone to hypnotize me, it would be to get skinny once and for all. Or maybe to quit smoking.

But I needed a different kind of help. I needed to stop flinching every time I heard his last name. I needed to stop leaving my body every time I passed a street sign that bore it.

Her office was small. Cozy. She had a line of colorful cigarette lighters displayed on a shelf like trophies. I figured they were from clients who'd quit. I took it as proof she was good at this. And I really needed her to be good at this.

I lay on the chaise and told her why I was there. Not the whole story. Just enough.

"I just moved to Denver. The guy who raped me my freshman year in college—his last name is the name of that street, and every time I hear his name"—which was everywhere, and she knew it too—"I go back there in my mind. And I need you to make it stop."

She nodded. And we got to work.

Turns out I'm one of those people who gets hypnotized easily. I dropped into a trance fast. But I could still hear her. I could still respond.

"Can you think of a place where you feel relaxed and calm?"

"I don't know . . . a picnic?" I love picnics.

She asked me about my favorite one. I told her about my college graduation party, the day my then-pregnant sister-in-law, Blanca, started having contractions and a few hours later my first nephew, David, was born. One of my favorite memories of all time.

The hypnotist went with it. Took the tenderness of that day, the day David was born, and wrapped it around the name that made my skin crawl.

And somehow, by magic and science (maybe both), it worked. Thank God, for several years, it worked.

For a good stretch, whenever I heard his last name, I thought of picnics, cake, celebration, my brother David and my sweet nephew who was named after him. That recalibration held strong for a while. One single session had transformed a trigger into something that no longer held me captive.

But what I thought was permanent wasn't. Gradually, the old associations crept back in. Still, that experience showed me something crucial: Our beliefs aren't as permanent as we think. If they can be installed, they can be uninstalled, even if it takes multiple tries.

For years, I thought the solution to trauma was to become invisible, to hide so well that nothing could ever again hurt me. But healing wasn't about disappearing. It was about reclaiming my right to exist fully in the world, triggers and all.

Those cultural taboos that feel unchangeable, and rules that feel like part of our genetic code, are all just programs running in the background of our minds.

What was written can be rewritten. What feels set in stone is actually more like sand. Even our deepest beliefs are just stories we've been telling ourselves for so long we forget we made them up.

I'd spent decades believing that staying hidden was the only way to stay safe. But the real safety came from learning we can handle whatever surfaces and we don't have to disappear every time life gets uncomfortable.

That session didn't erase what happened. But it rewired the part of me that kept reliving it. The hypnotherapy targeted one specific trigger, but the deeper patterns—the instinct to make myself smaller, to disappear when things got uncomfortable, to hide behind whatever I could find—those were still very much alive.

The real work of healing was just beginning.

But sometimes healing doesn't happen in therapy sessions or contemplative moments of self-reflection. Sometimes it happens in the most unexpected places.

You know about the documentary; I shared with you about that first screening in New York. But there's a piece of that story I've never shared, the part that almost made me walk away from the whole thing.

For seventeen years, I'd dreamed of making a documentary about the first-generation Latino experience. This persistent vision wouldn't leave me alone—the story I felt desperate to tell but never believed I was qualified to tell.

When I finally pitched the film, I positioned myself safely behind the camera. I'd interview other people, tell other people's stories. That felt manageable. That felt as if I could stay hidden while still serving the message.

Then my creative partner, an Oscar-nominated producer, looked me in the eye and said something that horrified me: "You should be the subject. Your personal story can carry this film."

Everything in me wanted to say no. I wasn't in the best shape. I didn't look polished enough. I believed in my imperfections more than I believed in my story's power. But here was someone who saw something in me that I couldn't see in myself.

We were already in production. There was no time to lose twenty pounds or get a perfect wardrobe or wait until I felt ready. I had a choice to make: indulge my belief in my smallness, or trust that my purpose was bigger than my self-doubt.

I chose the film.

I chose the message.

I chose to show up imperfectly rather than not show up at all.

Standing in front of that camera for the first time, I felt every cell in my body wanting to hide. But I also felt something powerful that had been buried under years of believing I wasn't enough. The same part of me that knew this story mattered more than my discomfort with how I looked telling it.

That film became my most powerful act yet of reclaiming divine beauty. I'd been practicing in small doses—buying myself flowers, refusing to demolish myself in the mirror—but when you say yes to what calls you despite your fear, the healing accelerates.

And it worked not because I looked perfect on camera, but because I honored what was sacred in me—my story, my purpose, my refusal to let fear win.

The potential impact of the film mattered more to me than indulging my belief in my limitations.

The revelation that followed blew my mind. If you feel called to do something bigger than what you believe you have the capacity to do, the pursuit of that thing will heal you. The film didn't just tell a story about first-generation identity—it reattached me to my divinity, weaving me back together with the sacred self I'd forgotten I was.

That breakthrough opened a door, but walking through it every day is the real work.

Even now, I still notice when my body tightens around being noticed. Because the truth is, Boston didn't teach me to hide; it just confirmed what I'd already learned from watching the world around me.

These lessons don't always come from what happens to us directly. Sometimes we learn them from watching—seeing Ana get judged for that bikini, watching successful women get called "bossy" or "aggressive" for the same behavior that makes men "leaders."

When Trauma Drives the Bus

The conference invitation arrives. Five thousand people. My biggest stage yet. And instead of celebrating, I'm standing in my closet at 2:00 a.m., trying on every outfit I own, hating how I look in all of them. I had let myself go—bad habits, stress eating, whatever. Part of me was okay with it because it felt safer to blend in, to not draw attention, to heed the warnings I'd grown up hearing about being "too much." But standing there in that harsh fluorescent light, I realized I was paying a different price. I didn't recognize myself or feel powerful in all this hiding.

That's when I remember something I'd written about La Mujer Divina. I put my hand on my heart, this body that had carried two children, survived trauma, built a career, made a film that mattered. "This body houses something sacred," I say to my reflection.

It doesn't erase the criticism. It doesn't make me suddenly love what I see. But for just a moment, I choose to honor the divine in me instead of tearing myself down. It is the smallest act of reclamation, but it is something.

By morning, I've convinced myself I'm not ready. I'm not worthy. I need to lose fifteen pounds first. The weight felt like my shame made visible, but losing it felt even more dangerous—like removing the last wall between me and a world that might devour me whole.

We create barriers to feel safe, then hate ourselves for needing them, then feel terrified to remove them. It's trauma's cruelest paradox.

This is what happens when our unhealed wounds are behind the wheel. Doesn't matter how impressive things look from the outside, if the scared teenager in you is calling the shots, everything still feels fragile. You know this feeling, when success should feel like celebration but instead feels like waiting for the other shoe to drop.

But it was during the film tour that the pattern became impossible to ignore.

I'm getting dressed for another conference, pulling on that same navy blue blazer that's gotten me through countless events this year. In the hotel mirror, I barely recognize myself. When did I start choosing clothes that camouflaged me?

When did "professional" become code for "please look right through me"? I realized I'd perfected the art of hiding in plain sight. Standing on stages in front of thousands, but dressed as if I were trying to disappear. Success was supposed to make me more confident, but instead it activated old beliefs about visibility being dangerous.

I felt trapped in a cycle I couldn't break. The more successful I became, the more I felt like hiding.

I need to clarify something important: This isn't about bigger bodies being wrong or smaller bodies being better. This was about my using weight as a hiding mechanism. When the world feels overwhelming, my body responds by creating more of itself—more padding, more protection, more distance between me and perceived danger. It happens so gradually I don't notice until my clothes stop fitting. The weight shields me, but it also makes me feel like a stranger to myself. For me, getting bigger was how I made myself less visible when the world felt too overwhelming.

I have clothes for every version of my body that spans four to five different sizes. At any given time I can only wear about 15 percent of my wardrobe, as I mostly choose whatever feels stretchy and soft against my skin.

Society and our shared upbringing supported my disappearing act.

In our culture, we're taught to put everyone's needs before our own—be the perfect caretaker, the selfless mother, the one who holds it all together. But we're also expected to never "let ourselves go," to somehow maintain our bodies while we juggle everyone else's needs. It's a lose-lose standard that sets us up for self-abandonment.

As a Latina mother and wife, I was trained from a young age to put everyone else first. Taking care of myself, such as prioritizing my health, my well-being, creating boundaries, having rituals that honored who I was, felt impossible. Self-care was acceptable in theory, but only as long as it didn't interfere with family obligations. Spend too much time on yourself and you risk being seen as selfish.

The weight was just the visible evidence of a woman who had abandoned herself completely.

I'm standing in Target holding a cute dress, and my daughter tugs at my cart. "Mommy, can we go?" I put the dress back. My mind instantly floods with rationalizations to numb the sting. Forty-nine dollars can buy her new soccer cleats instead. I convince myself that if I really love it, I can find it online later, or when there's a sale. It wasn't about the fabric or the design, it was just Target, but it was new, and I hadn't touched "new" in ages. The fantasy version of me was the mom who'd actually made it to the gym at 6 a.m. that morning. The woman putting it back looked like the one who'd given up.

Walking to the car, I felt a sudden burn of chafing between my legs. The Lycra had thinned out, eroded by the friction of a life spent in motion for everyone else—emptying the dishwasher for the umpteenth time, throwing in yet another load of laundry, making three different dinners because no one likes the same thing.

You don't feel the fabric pilling until it rips. That sting reminded me of running 5Ks, when I used to move because I loved my body. Now the sting just signaled that I was further gone than I realized.

I don't have time to work out; the kids need me.

I can't afford new clothes, we're saving for their college, and I don't fit in the clothes I want to wear anyway.

I'll focus on myself once things slow down.

I told myself these were just excuses. But really? This was how I'd learned to hide.

The scared teenager who learned that being seen meant being hurt had found the perfect adult disguise, the selfless one. We're praised for abandoning ourselves as long as we're "being a good mother."

If you're putting everyone else's needs first while your own dreams collect dust, you're disappearing too. And we don't need you small, we need you fully alive.

I let parenting and life's obligations win the day instead of me winning my day. And everyone praised me for it.

It was the same pattern I'd learned as a teenager: When life felt unsafe, I made myself invisible. Only now I was being practical, being a good mom and being responsible. But underneath all those noble reasons, I was still that scared girl who believed shrinking was safer than shining.

The Perfect Hiding Place

The scared part of me that learned beauty and being noticed were risky had found the perfect hiding place in raising a family, where being a martyr can so easily be mistaken for love.

I understood suddenly: I had become my mother.

The very thing I swore I'd never be, the woman who vanished into everyone else's needs, who made herself smaller so others could be comfortable, who wore her suffering like a badge of honor, that was me.

The Photograph

It was during that difficult summer of 2024, while packing boxes and dealing with the aftermath of everything falling apart, that I found it, a photograph I'd forgotten I had tucked in a folder. Me at sixteen, on the deck of a boat sailing from Spain to Morocco. Navy bathing suit, sunglasses purchased from a street vendor in Centro Histórico in Málaga, wearing my favorite lip gloss I wore that whole summer—#44, this frosty light pink that my whole friend group bought at Rexall Drugs and wore religiously—a book in my hands, confident and radiant.

I wasn't posing for this photograph. There was no angling for the perfect shot, no checking my hair, no asking to see it before anyone else could. Just a photographer capturing a moment in a picture I didn't even know was being taken. A girl reading on a boat, completely absorbed in her book and her adventure, unaware of the camera and utterly comfortable in her own skin.

I remembered exactly how I felt in that moment—gorgeous, powerful, as fluent in Spanish as I've ever been, surrounded by friends from all over Europe, having paid for this weekend excursion to Africa myself. Every box was ticked. I was everything I wanted to be, at any age.

As I stare at that image, there's no other way to see myself but radiant. The divinity I hadn't yet discovered was already there, in the way I held my body, in my complete presence, in the joy radiating from someone who was simply living her life fully.

She was still in me; I'd just forgotten her.

Life has a way of doing that—each crisis, each disappointment, each moment we choose endurance over joy slowly erodes our connection to that radiant self. We let the hard times define us instead of remembering they're just moments. We forget that magic was never dependent on perfect circumstances.

Looking at that photograph, I felt something wild and familiar stir inside me. She wasn't gone! She was just buried under years of believing my power was unacceptable. The comeback wasn't about becoming someone new; it was unleashing who I'd always been.

That photograph became my North Star. A reminder of who I was when I wasn't afraid of my own light. And nowhere was that clearer than when I returned to one of my favorite stages.

The Ritual

Before I speak onstage (if possible), I find a secluded place—sometimes it's in a greenroom or a bathroom, sometimes it's while I'm leaning against the door I'm about to walk through—and place my open hand over my heart. That simple gesture, palm to chest, reminds me that I'm not just a mind or a voice. I'm a vessel. And I need all of me to show up.

This is how I tether my mind, body, and spirit together. This is how I get myself in the moment.

It sounds small, but it's now as instinctual to me as breathing. Like when I ask my dog, Cookie, if she wants to go for a walk—instant spark. Tail wagging, body vibrating with excitement, her little chocolate-chip eyes laser focused on mine. That's what this gesture does for me. It's a signal to my system saying, *We're doing something important now, so wake up and be here fully.*

Being present isn't just mental. If you've ever floated through a moment nodding, smiling, but somehow not in your body, you know what I mean. This ritual brings me back to earth. Back to myself. And when I'm about to walk onstage and give myself fully, I need every part of me present.

Then, I say the prayer:

> *God,*
> *Give me the perfect words to say,*
> *With the perfect timing,*
> *And in the perfect way.*

That prayer reminds me that I need to trust that what's meant to come through me will.

I don't remember exactly when I started doing this. I do remember the anxiety and rush of impossible nerves before every keynote, when my thoughts scattered away from my message and my breath got caught in my throat more times than I'd like to admit. For a long time, I powered through it (story of my life). Then one day, I tried something different. Hand to heart, a few deep breaths, and my soft prayer. It worked. So, I kept going. And over time, it became sacred.

Now, I use this ritual whenever I need that level of trust. When I feel nervous. When something feels bigger than me. When I want to get out of my head and embody my knowing.

And the moment I say that prayer, something shifts. My feet feel heavy and rooted under me in the best of ways. My breath slows, my mind gets clear, and the noise fades.

I'm not "performing" a keynote like a monologue anymore. Instead, I'm offering, I'm present, and I'm powerful.

And then there were the velvet pants, my literal declaration that I was finally ready to celebrate myself.

The Woman in Velvet

Years ago, I had spoken to Lean In Latinas in the Bay Area. Out of more than four hundred speaking engagements over nine years, that room full of Latinas had quickly become one of my absolute favorites. When the opportunity came to return to them after everything I'd been through, the business collapse, the complete upheaval of my life, it felt as if the universe was offering me exactly what I needed.

As I walked toward the stage, something felt different. I had my usual pre-keynote nerves, but for the first time I wasn't fighting them. I was nervous *and* confident, which felt like a miracle.

As I shared my message, one I'd spent considerable time customizing for them, I could see it was landing. Everything was becoming clear. I felt deeply grateful, definitely touching the divine, definitely in my sacred power.

Earlier that summer I was questioning if I was even good at this anymore. But standing on that stage, sharing my message with so much joy, I knew I was exactly where I belonged.

I don't expect standing ovations, no speaker does. They happen occasionally, and when they do, you feel fortunate. At the end of my keynote, I took two steps back, raised and stretched both arms out on each side, palms open and facing the audience, and said, "Thank you so much," and began making my way offstage.

I turned toward them to take in the moment and get one last look at these extraordinary people who helped me more in those forty minutes than they'll ever know. And when I did, I noticed the entire room was standing. Every single person.

Something had shifted. I hadn't realized how all this inner work might translate professionally, but there I was in my full authentic beauty, my true power, reflected back to me in their faces.

Standing there in a simple denim shirt and navy pencil skirt, I thought about all the other times, all the hotel mirrors, where I'd barely recognized myself, swimming in those shapeless dresses I chose because they fit whether I'm fifteen pounds heavier or lighter—the ultimate hiding uniform. Those navy blazers covered even more, making me look practical and "professional" instead of powerful in my true self.

What I really want to be wearing are my dark plum velvet pants. I remember opening them on my birthday, the sound of tissue paper crinkling as I broke the metallic sticker elegantly holding both sides of the wrapping together. The velvet was heavy, dense, and luxurious. Under the dim light of my bedroom they flashed a rich regal purple, the same color as an eggplant, mysterious and fine. My fingers glided over the nap; it felt like sinking into a plush rug. They were made with good fabric that doesn't pill or thin out.

But they didn't fit. I knew it the moment I held the rigid waist in front of me. This fabric had no give, not like the forgiving Lycra I loved to live in. I wrapped the waist around my neck—the telltale sign if they would work or not, and the ends did not meet. I tried them on anyway, desperate for the dream to be real, but they seized up midthigh. A hard stop and I was crushed.

They're still folded in that tissue paper inside that beautiful box, but suddenly I realize that woman isn't going to wait for these pants to fit; she's waiting for me to claim her.

The woman who electrifies rooms with her power and truth—she doesn't need perfect conditions. She takes her fears with her and shows up anyway. She wears velvet not because she's fearless, but because she's done hiding.

I'm going to wear those pants on my book tour—whether they fit perfectly or not. Because writing this book *is* my healing. Sharing these stories *is* my purpose. And the woman who can transform lives through her vulnerability has been here all along, waiting for me patiently in stunning plum velvet.

She rediscovers power in her divinity.

Reflection

The velvet pants aren't waiting for me to become someone new. They're waiting for me to accept that I can be confident in my message and still get nervous before I deliver it. That the woman who flinches at street names and the woman who rocks stages and captivates audiences of thousands can coexist in the same body, in the same moment, in the same breath.

Exercise: Your Beautiful Contradictions

When we stop trying to be perfect and start embracing our multitudes, we finally access our true essence, which comes from being fully authentically ourselves.

PART ONE: THE BEAUTIFUL TRUTH

Think of two seemingly contradictory truths about yourself. Maybe you're confident about your work, but still nervous before big meetings, or powerful in your purpose but still uncertain about your next steps. Now place your hand on your heart and wait until you can feel it beating. Take a deep breath and then say out loud, "I can be confident about _______________ and still _______________ at the same time."

PART TWO: DISCOVERING YOUR DIVINE BEAUTY

I've learned that our most radiant moments aren't when we are perfect; they are when we are fully ourselves.

Now, ask yourself: "What feels magnetic to *me* right now? Not what other people think is beautiful, but what makes *me* feel radiant and alive?"

Maybe it's the way you move when you're dancing and singing in your kitchen or how your eyes light up when you're passionate about something. The way you express yourself with your whole body when something genuinely excites you.

Say it out loud: "I feel most alive when I ____________________."

Notice how your body responds when you give yourself permission to hold both truths—your contradictions *and* your beauty. This integration isn't about becoming perfect; it's about you feeling whole.

The magic happens when you realize the moments you feel most alive are probably the moments you're not trying to be perfect. You're just being gloriously, messily, authentically you. Write both statements on sticky notes for your bathroom mirror. Claim your contradictions and your beauty because *they are the same thing.*

CHAPTER SIX

Don't Dishonor Your Mother:

How to Prioritize Your Own Healing over Fixing Tu Madre

In our families, mothers are like superheroes. We're providers, warriors, expert chefs, storytellers, culture bearers, curanderas, and caregivers to everyone—from our abuelitos to our neighbors to our communities at large. We put our own needs and struggles aside to provide for everyone else. What stands out about our style of motherhood is the way we love and the lessons we pass down.

But sometimes, the burden we bear is too heavy for any one person to hold, and the methods we choose to wield it don't make sense anymore.

This weight is real. And as a Latina mother myself, I'm proud of how our Latinidad shapes the way we love our children. But sometimes the weight we carry (and pass down) becomes too much, and that's exactly what happened in my family.

This is *my* truth about that weight. Sadly, I know my mother will probably read this chapter and feel betrayed, even though I haven't written it yet. That's how well I know the sting of disappointing her.

This chapter wasn't easy to write. It's personal and raw and, for me, it might be the most important one in this book. Because I know I'm not the only daughter of a Latina mother who's carried pain she didn't cause. Who learned to swallow her needs to keep the peace. Who has desperately waited for someone to come save her while her mother modeled that strong women don't need saving.

I'm about to break every rule in the invisible Latina mother-daughter handbook. We don't talk about these things. Not in our culture. Not out loud. Not where others can hear, and especially not where others in our community can hear, because what would they say?

No more pretending that love and loyalty mean harboring our pain alone until it becomes part of our identity. I'm not offering you easy answers here. I am offering you the truth. And if you're willing, I want us to walk into these dark spaces together—not to stay there for too long, but to see what might be waiting for us on the other side.

They say the truth sets you free. But first, it effing hurts.

And then, it liberates.

That liberation didn't come easy for me because I used to think I owed my mother everything. That somehow I was responsible for her suffering, her sadness, her disappointment. And I held it all. What she passed down wasn't jewelry or property. It was shame. Guilt. All the things I learned not to talk about.

Here's what that looked like in real life. . . .

The Art of Silent Suffering

I was on the longest conference call of my life when I felt it, the warm blood seeping through my underwear, threatening to leave a permanent mark on my office chair's textured tweed upholstery. The warmth is familiar to anyone who bleeds, almost soothing if I didn't know it was about to ruin me. A memory of life, now signaling death.

I excused myself midsentence and speed-walked down the hall to the private bathroom, clenching my muscles and feeling blood dripping because it had nowhere else to go. I prayed my DIY pad would hold, the one I'd rigged together an hour earlier because God forbid I admit I needed to go home.

It had already soaked all the way through.

While sitting down on the toilet, it sprang out of my underwear and exploded into hundreds of blood-soaked shreds of toilet paper and scattered across the executive bathroom's pristine floor. Tiny rice-shaped bloody bits wedged in the white grout of the one-inch-by-one-inch ceramic tiles.

It was slick and clean, but the lines between were a porous trap for my blood. I knew for sure it would stain unless I scrubbed it out right then before it dried. I didn't know what shade of red it would leave behind.

With a stack of cheap wet bathroom paper hand towels I started cleaning with precision like I was detailing a car. Irritated because I didn't have the time I was taking to get the blood out, but I needed to get the blood out. I was so mad at myself for not being home, for not taking the day and for being on my knees erasing the blood from my bathroom floor while losing my baby.

I wanted to scream. But even then, I worried someone might hear me.

A week earlier, my ob-gyn had given it a neat little name, a "missed miscarriage." Somehow the word *missed* made it feel even more like my fault, like I'd forgotten to do something and that's why our baby had stopped growing at eight weeks, but my body, ever the good soldier, kept carrying her at ten.

I held on. *Story of my life.*

This devastated me for a million reasons, the first and hardest being that both my husband and I were already so in love with our unexpected bundle of joy. We kept looking at each other and giggling the way we did when I carried our girls.

Being pregnant again felt like a miracle. A second chance to relive those early baby years. The exhaustion, the brain fog, the sweetness. That time had shaped us as parents and partners. It reminded me that I hadn't just married an amazing man but a gentle, loving father too. This new baby felt like a surprise gift we didn't even know to ask for.

So when the bleeding started, I told myself it was probably nothing. But when the doctor confirmed the baby had stopped growing and that there was no heartbeat, I was devastated. A whole future, our wild dream of a family of five, like the ones we both came from, was gone.

It was a terrible time to be pregnant. It would've made life harder, more expensive, more complicated.

That's what we told ourselves.

And still, I went to work. I bled through all my grief onto that DIY pad, my blood now soaking the bathroom floor like some abstract art piece.

I should've been in bed. Or on the couch. Or curled up in a ball of sadness that matched the size of our loss. But asking for that kind of care didn't even occur to me. I never thought to say, "I'm not okay."

I didn't tell anyone at work I was bleeding. Didn't share I was grieving. I just cleaned up my bloody mess and kept going like my mother would have, like her mother before her. Because no one knew, they couldn't say, "Mija, go home, you need to rest," because if someone said that, I might have considered it.

I stayed silent. And kept going.

We needed the money, or at least that's what I told myself. Truth is, I've always chosen a paycheck over my well-being. Always said, "Yes," as if any given single opportunity might be my last. As if missing one day of work would make my whole life unravel.

Later when I had perspective and money in my checking account, I saw that I still lived and worked as if I were one month away from disaster. *I've never not been in survival mode.* I believed I was so needed that I couldn't imagine "doing that to them." Leaving, to take care of myself. Taking up that kind of space. As if somehow my pain was an inconvenience but my bleeding body at work was a gift I was giving to everyone else.

I didn't just misunderstand my value; I misunderstood the whole damn game.

Each time I chose to withdraw—at work, in relationships, in my own pain—I was making a choice. And once I saw that, it became clear that if I chose it, I could unchoose it.

"Working hard" was code for working myself to the bone. In my family, the most virtuous giving that got me those precious "Ay, qué buena hija" comments was when I came dead last. That's what I thought it meant to be a good woman.

Worthiness came with a price, disappearing bit by bit.

High praise always went to las mamis who gave the most, suffered the most, and never asked for anything in return. Well "Dios la bendiga" to them. They're treated like saints. Like real-life Virgin Marys.

They make suffering seem aspirational and holy and make life ten times harder for the rest of us.

Which is why my miscarriage plan looked like this:

Miscarry on Saturday.

Rest on Sunday (because even God took one day).

Back to work on Monday.

The Choice Not to Rest

That miscarriage wasn't the first time I'd chosen being agreeable over my own well-being. It wasn't even the first time my body had paid the price for putting everyone else's comfort before my own mental health.

When I was pregnant with my first daughter, at twenty-two weeks I was diagnosed with what my doctor, with a straight face, called an "incompetent cervix." It felt like a bad joke, like something made up to shame me for literally failing at being pregnant. My cervix was opening too soon. I was told I needed strict and total bed rest for the duration of the pregnancy.

They sewed my cervix shut with what the doctor described as medical-grade shoelaces, as if something so ordinary could hold a life together, and sent me home with prescriptions for two types of antiseizure meds, because one wasn't enough to stave off the contractions. I became a statue in my own bed. I learned to breathe from the top of my lungs only, panic-stricken that a deep exhale might untie the knot. My body wasn't mine anymore but instead a fragile container I was frightened to break. Every shift of the sheets felt like a gamble with a life. I could barely move without triggering a wave of contractions. Everything about my posture, my breathing, and, surprisingly, my thoughts had to stay calm lest they come back and get out of control. Worst-case scenario was the stitches would rip my cervix open, and I'd have my baby girl too soon to be kept alive. So strict bed rest it was.

We needed help, and my mother offered and flew in.

I'd worked myself up to asking her on the phone before she came to please not fight with me while she was here. That was the deal. I needed her support. Not the chaos that often came with her visits.

But the morning after she arrived, she plopped down at the foot of my bed and asked if there was any coffee. Then she asked what was for breakfast.

I was shocked because even then, after all the disappointments, all the evidence, I was still that daughter who believed in impossible transformations. Who thought maybe this time would be different with her. Maybe my personal medical crisis would break through to something new in her. Maybe my needs would finally teach her to really see me.

But there she sat at the foot of my bed, asking for coffee, and I felt that familiar disappointment of my hope collapsing.

This crisis was happening to me and no one else. This was my body holding on to her granddaughter by a thread, and still she expected me to serve her.

I told her I couldn't get out of bed to cook. That, yes, there was coffee, and could she please make some. I needed her to take over. That was why she was here, wasn't it?

She squinted at the blank space in front of her, confused.

"But I don't know where anything is in your kitchen," as if by stating this fact I could will my cervix to stay closed while I jumped up to give her a tour.

She pursed her lips and exhaled while looking out the window, as if I'd violated some unspoken law by not getting up to serve her.

A few days into her thankless job of helping us, things began to feel like a pressure cooker. She should have gone home then. I told her if making food and lounging around with me was too much, she could leave. This seemed to offend her. I *was* a little snarky about it.

She kept talking about feeling torn and missing my stepdad, wanting to be back home in New York, but knowing I needed her. As if she were working out some impossible math problem. But it wasn't complicated to me at all. I was twenty-two weeks pregnant, scared out of my mind, and I needed my mom. At home, she could worry about me from a distance, make phone calls, tell people about her daughter's crisis. But here she had to actually sit with me, day after day, and she couldn't do it.

Her voice changed, to that familiar irritation I'd known my whole life. Quickly, a simple conversation erupted into a full-blown argument. I begged her to stop, my contractions spiraling out of control. But she was caught in her own pain, unable to see mine, and I realized this pattern had shaped our relationship, her wounds always taking up more space than my healing. I cried while my uterus contracted as if I'd taken no medication at all. I was certain the stitches were ripping, but still, she wouldn't leave my room.

She even corrected my language, insisting this wasn't "arguing," it was just "tension." Either way, it devoured my energy and demolished my reserves. It seemed as if she wanted me out of bed, moving, as if I was lying there by choice. As if my bed rest were a mild depression or drama or attention seeking.

We were speaking in code. The kind others wouldn't understand. She never got really mean when other people were around. That part she reserved for me.

Every breath, every sigh, every eye roll, utterly loaded. We were always just one comment, one weird look, away from an explosion.

I felt trapped.

Trapped in my bedroom, the space I'd built for peace, with the person who could take it away with a single sigh. And still, she expected to be treated like a guest.

When she left for her home, I felt as if I had survived something more dangerous than the high-risk pregnancy.

We don't talk about this in our families, how our mothers' inability to center anyone but themselves could literally become a medical emergency. How their need to be served, even when we're fighting to keep a baby alive, isn't just selfishness but a trauma response they learned from their own mothers. But acknowledging it feels like the ultimate betrayal.

But that wasn't the end.

Years later, after both of my daughters were born, we were living in a loft in downtown Denver, sitting on stools by the kitchen island, scrolling through pictures from a recent fundraiser for my film. My mother and aunt were visiting. The vibe was neutral, a surface-level calm.

Until my daughter Georgina, eight years old and radiant, interrupted us.

Just a child being a child. Loud and curious.

She wanted my mother's attention, but I wanted to keep it, a secret hunger I'd carried my whole life.

I asked my mom to please just keep sitting with me, with the pictures, just a bit longer. I was so proud of my work and of this film I was working on, which could help thousands feel less alone.

But she couldn't stay in that moment with me. My daughter's attention was too tempting. It was what she wanted next. A child's attention is pure, uncomplicated. No history, no baggage, no expectations she might fail to meet. My eight-year-old wasn't asking her to be different or better, just to be present. With me, there was always the weight of our history, the unspoken strain of all the ways we'd hurt each other. Maybe it was easier to be needed by a child than to be seen by an adult daughter who had lived through it all with her. Georgina offered her a clean slate, a chance to be the grandmother she could never quite figure out how to be as a mother—without the messy history that made our connection feel so fraught.

It took me time to see that for those few minutes I had been centered, and those types of moments could never last longer than a few minutes.

The fight erupted just moments later. The trigger was my asking for her attention when she was done giving it. Not acceptable. She was storming again, and I was again the eye of it.

I wish I could tell you exactly what was said, but I can't. My brain learned long ago not to store the specifics of these moments—the nonsensical accusations, the way my simple request would get twisted into evidence of my fundamental badness. It was as if we'd both flip into a mode where pain lived just under the surface, ready to combust at lightning speed. Afterward I'd have this strange amnesia, as if my mind could protect me by refusing to hold on to the chaos.

What I remember instead are sensations, the familiar knot in my stomach, the way the air in the room changed, the feeling of being pulled into a vortex and pinned there by its centrifugal force. The content of our fights mattered less than the dynamic, how quickly love could turn to warfare, how easily I could become the problem that needed solving.

When I pointed this out—"Mami, Georgie can wait just a few minutes while we finish looking at the pictures"—she stood up abruptly.

"I can't breathe," she said, grabbing her chest. "My heart . . ."

Her breathing became labored and dramatic.

"Are you okay? What's happening?" I asked, immediately shifting into crisis mode.

The transformation was instant—from irritated to total breakdown in seconds. There was no part of this moment that didn't feel like an act, though I'm sure to her it felt completely real.

The response was so familiar, though it had never before been medical. When attention shifted away from her, even for a few moments, her body would respond with sighing, shifting, disconnecting, walking away. But this time it escalated to heart palpitations, difficulty breathing, dehydration. A new level of the same old pattern of reclaiming center stage.

Somehow, my asking for a few more minutes had triggered what felt to her like a medical emergency. The disconnect between what I'd said and what she'd experienced was heartbreaking.

I switched gears from the pictures and guided her to my daughter's bedroom, onto the bottom bunk, and called urgent care. A nurse answered and within minutes identified the issue, altitude sickness, something we hadn't considered.

My mother then asked to be left alone. Soon she and my aunt began packing and left Denver earlier than planned. I felt relief, but also profound sadness. Her early exit felt like another abandonment—hers of me, and mine of any hope that we could be different together.

That visit was followed by a letter. It came by email first, then again by physical mail on the same day. Printed and formal, like a business transaction.

Her language was clinical. Her tone was final. But I had already begun to grieve our relationship long before her message arrived. I was awake to our pattern, to my role and to hers.

She told me that nothing she could do would fix my "anger and strong feelings" against her and that my actions were disrespectful. She had decided to "step back" and remove herself from my life. Most painful of all, she asked me to never share anything about my documentary with her again.

I'm not sharing this part of her letter to call her out. She's a respected and beloved figure in her community. But she's also the person who wrote this letter. I tell this story as a reckoning with the complicated, messy human ways we hurt each other in families, often without meaning to. She may never see it this way. And that's okay. I'm not writing this to change her. I'm writing this to free myself and to help free you too.

I believe our story reflects a system of emotional control, hierarchy, and unspoken rules where love is conditional and truth is taboo. My mother passed down what was given to her. I'm the one choosing to end it.

The clinical tone, the way my simple request became "anger and strong feelings," the request to be excluded from my life's work—she was using therapy language to hurt me.

The demand that cut deepest was about my film. My mother could never handle the theme. She seemed to think I would spend the entire film criticizing her, so she showed little curiosity and even less interest. When she asked to be excluded from "anything related to the documentary," she was rejecting the thing that meant everything to me.

The film went on to become successful worldwide. Not just with Latino audiences, but with children of immigrants from many countries—people who understood that specific loneliness, that universal struggle of never feeling that they were enough. It launched my speaking career, leading to over four hundred stages and ultimately this book.

Even after the film's global success, during screenings I caught her whispering corrections to audience members about details she felt I'd gotten wrong, all of them about her.

Her age when she moved here from PR, small factual details about her story. She wanted distance from my success, but she still wanted control over how I told our story. When I finally asked her to stop, she just looked at me and said nothing. Shaping the narrative mattered more than supporting her daughter.

If you found yourself wanting to protect someone while reading this, if you felt that familiar "What will they say?" voice creeping in . . . that's the spell.

This whole book is designed to break it.

In our culture, *obedience* is a spell. It's cast early and woven into what feels like love. It sounds like "familia first," but it keeps you small.

Sometimes it makes you wonder:

Maybe I misread this.

Maybe I overreacted.

What will people think or say?

Am I betraying her by telling the truth?

When you tell the truth, you do something else too. You break the family code of silence that's been handed down for generations.

Because every time a Latina daughter feels something painful and then immediately thinks—*But I can't say that. What will they think of her? What will they think of me?*—the intergenerational contract of secrecy tightens its grip.

Resistance to sharing doesn't mean the story isn't meant to be told. Consider that the resistance is the proof that it's been buried too long.

So, yes, this shame has roots. How many times were we told "Don't speak ill of your elders," and how many times were we made to feel wrong for being "too sensitive"?

It's the fear of being the first one to say what no one else dares say. And that's why this matters.

It would take a decade from this point for me to fully accept that my mom could never be the mother I desperately ached for. That no amount of self-hatred and kowtowing to her needs, pretending to be captivated by her many accomplishments, would ever make her capable of being what I needed. Even so, her letter shattered something inside me I didn't know could break.

I don't think I've ever cried that hard.

That day I felt something die between us, and our relationship was never the same. Whenever I chose her peace over my truth, I paid a price and I sacrificed a little more of myself, every time.

Every story in this chapter—the bed rest, the dehydration, her letter—they were all drops in an ocean I was drowning in.

My body and my spirit remembered, and the ache was impossible to ignore. But when I held my daughter for the first time, I felt hopeful and grateful for another chance.

When I named her Georgina, I wasn't trying to replicate anything. But maybe you could say I was trying to reclaim something that the rupture had stolen from me, the possibility of what mother-daughter love could actually feel like.

What Inheritance Do You Want to Leave?

My mother always talked about her mother, Georgina, as if their relationship were perfect.

She would describe her as generous, wonderful, patient, kind. She went out of her way to paint their relationship as extraordinary, telling me repeatedly how much she respected her mother, how

Georgina made all the right decisions and what a selfless woman she was.

She never actually said Georgina was "the epitome of everything a mother should be," but she certainly took every opportunity to hint at it. Which in and of itself would be fine, except there was always some kind of comment in there that made me feel that we weren't talking about how wonderful Georgina was—we were talking about how terrible I was. Somehow the subtext always got through.

She never said directly, "I would never have spoken to my mother the way you speak to me." She was more clever than that. Instead, she'd paint this picture of herself as the respectful daughter who never questioned, never pushed back, never made things difficult. I was good at reading between the lines: This is what a good daughter looks like. Got it.

Meanwhile, I was the daughter who asked a gazillion questions, who wanted to understand things, had my own opinions, was developing the beginnings of boundaries, which seemed unacceptable in our house. When I heard these stories about their flawless relationship over and over, I started believing I was the reason our relationship couldn't be like theirs and there was something fundamentally shameful within me.

In our culture, this reverence for mothers is expected and unquestionable. Mothers are meant to be these saintly, untouchable figures, and daughters are supposed to aspire to that same unrealistic standard.

My mother would go on and on about how close they were, how much she revered her, how she would never have dared to go against her.

"I *always* trusted my mother's judgment, even when I disagreed with her" or "I *always* gave my mother the benefit of the doubt." And as a child, I believed every word. That became the effect, I think, because I felt like the problem.

As if I were the damaged one in a lineage of perfect daughters.

My curiosity became "too many questions." My developing boundaries became "disrespectful." My opinions became evidence that I was difficult to parent. Meanwhile, she'd describe how Georgina never had to worry about any of this with her because she was naturally obedient, naturally compliant, naturally grateful for everything her mother did.

I carried the weight of that comparison deep in my body. *What's wrong with me?* I wondered while listening to her share about her relationship with my grandmother Georgina.

But to understand what cycle I was actually trying to break free from, I had to go back to the beginning. To the original Georgina's story . . .

The Myth and the Rebellion

My mother carried grief that felt too big for one person to hold. Pain from her childhood, patterns she'd inherited without ever examining them. But instead of processing that pain, she needed me to carry it with her. Her needs, her grief, her sadness, her anger, always came first in importance. This was never in question. It was just how things were, and I accepted it 100 percent.

I became her emotional caretaker before I even understood what emotions were. Her pain became my responsibility to soothe. Her moods became my weather system to navigate. My job was to make her feel better, not to have feelings of my own.

What I failed to understand then was that this wasn't just about my mother and me. This was about a century-old survival strategy that had kept us stuck.

Every time she shared stories about her flawless bond with her mother, she was unconsciously reinforcing a rule: This is what good daughters do. They sacrifice everything and ask for nothing. They fix their mothers' lives through their own surrender.

Being simpática meant I was supposed to bite my tongue when she created chaos, even when my contractions spiked from the stress. Asking her to stop arguing wasn't just disrespectful, it was a fundamental failure of what good daughters do. We don't engage in conflict, we don't call out behavior, we absorb.

But I couldn't do it. Something in me kept refusing to comply.

Each time I pushed back, I could feel her disappointment. Not just in my behavior, but in my unwillingness to be the daughter she needed me to be. The daughter who would make her life as effortless as she claimed hers had been with her mother.

I was labeled "difficult" because I couldn't master the art of making myself smaller. "Rebellious" because I kept asking for things—rest, peace, consideration. "A problem" because I refused to carry her emotional chaos while my body was trying to hold on to my daughter.

This pattern didn't stay contained to that bedroom. It followed me everywhere.

At work, bleeding through a miscarriage, I wouldn't even consider asking to go home. The pressure to be simpática had taught me that my pain was always secondary to everyone else's comfort. I couldn't take care of myself without feeling selfish, like an inconvenience I was imposing on others.

In relationships, I became the eternal emotional caretaker, the one who managed everyone else's moods and dysregulation. I learned to read the room with a hypervigilance that lived deep in my nervous system. Growing up, my mother's emotional frequency was the barometer that determined whether our house was calm or unsettled.

I said yes to everything—projects, requests, demands on my time—because familismo had wired me to believe that my worth came from how much I could give and how little I could need. The phrase *Ay, qué buena hija* was like a drug. I chased that approval by disappearing piece by piece.

But my body kept rebelling. Panic attacks when I tried to be perfect. Exhaustion I couldn't shake. A voice inside me that wouldn't shut up, no matter how much I tried to drown it out.

The shame was crushing. Why couldn't I just be grateful? Why can't we just serve without resentment? Why do we keep wanting things like the right to have feelings that aren't about managing someone else's crisis?

I felt defective. Like there was something wrong with me that I couldn't live up to what seemed to come so naturally to the women in my family, the art of holy suffering and of making everyone else's life better by making mine smaller.

Back then, I had no idea my rebellion wasn't something that was wrong with me. It was my soul rejecting trauma that wasn't mine to hold.

I thought I was the only one struggling with this impossible standard. I thought there was something flawed about me that I couldn't just disappear gracefully the way a good daughter should. Turns out, 76 percent of Latinas are doing exactly what I was doing, hiding parts of themselves in professional settings to avoid being "too much."[1] We've been so conditioned to make ourselves smaller that we do it automatically, even in spaces where our full selves are exactly what's needed.

Latina women make up a disproportionate share of unpaid family caregivers in the United States.[2] We're more likely to experience workplace burnout[3] but less likely to seek therapy because asking for help feels like a moral failure.[4] We've been taught that good women suffer in silence.

The cultural message is clear: Pursuing demanding careers or education can be perceived as a deviation from our role as eternal caregivers, leading to internal conflict and guilt. We're *supposed* to feel selfish for wanting more than a life of service.

This isn't something wrong with us individually. This is a systematic cultural pattern that teaches daughters that their worth comes from how much they can sacrifice, how little they can require, how perfectly they can disappear to make everyone else's life easier.

The relationship my mother described with her own mother came at the cost of my grandmother's complete self-erasure. She learned to carry pain that wasn't hers, to erase her needs, to make her daughter's life perfect by making her own invisible.

And my mother, steeped in that model, expected me to do the same. When I couldn't, when I kept pushing back, it felt like a betrayal of everything she'd learned about what love looks like.

But here's what the research also shows: This pattern of self-sacrifice that we've been taught to see as virtue is actually a trauma response,[5] passed down through generations of women who had no other choice.[6]

To understand how deep this pattern runs, I had to go back to the beginning. To my grandmother's story.

A few years ago, I worked with a genealogist to research our family history. What she uncovered revealed a much more complicated truth.

My grandmother had started as a boarder in my grandfather's household when she was very young—likely sent there by her poor family to work as a maid for this wealthier family, which was common at the time. While living there, she met and fell in love with a man named Santiago. They were so young when they married that they needed special permission from the Church.

A few years later, Santiago disappears—my genealogist thinks he either died or may have left my grandmother for another woman, since there's no death certificate to confirm it. My grandmother reappears back at that same address, the records showing her once again with my grandfather and his wife.

This was the early 1900s. Catholic doctrine meant she couldn't remarry after Santiago. So, when she ended up having seven children with my grandfather (who had already been married), she was trapped in an unthinkable situation. She couldn't legally marry him, but she had nowhere else to go.

My grandfather had a history of violent jealousy—a volatility that could turn deadly when he believed his honor was at stake. Yet for my grandmother, returning to his household—after his wife was no longer in the picture—represented the safest option available to a woman who had been failed by both the Church and the system.

What my mother missed, what she couldn't see, was that my grandmother's "extraordinary" devotion wasn't born from pure love. It was born from necessity.

A young woman with seven children and no legal marriage had no other choice but to be beyond reproach. She *had* to embody every aspect of marianismo flawlessly and become the ultimate caretaker (familismo), never causing conflict (simpática), maintaining moral purity despite her impossible situation (respeto), just to survive the social stigma of her circumstances.

My grandmother couldn't afford to have needs. She couldn't afford to question. She couldn't afford to be anything less than saintly because her entire existence depended on proving her moral worth to a community that saw her as living in sin.

So, she became the perfect wife, the perfect woman, the perfect mother. Not because it felt good, but because it kept her alive.

My mother, witnessing this level of devotion, likely internalized it as the gold standard of love. Good daughters sacrifice everything. Good daughters never question. Love meant complete self-sacrifice.

But breaking these rules can feel disloyal, especially to the person who taught them to you as care.

I can't know what my grandmother felt in her heart. I can't know if she found joy despite her circumstances, or if she suffered privately, or if she made peace with a life she never chose.

What I do know is that the circumstances she navigated required her to be flawless just to get by. She'd lost her first love, Santiago, and found herself back in my grandfather's household. While having children outside of legal marriage wasn't uncommon in Puerto Rico at the time, it still carried social weight. And at some point, she made what must have been a difficult decision to leave Catholicism and become Presbyterian.

Maybe she changed religions to find a community that judged her less. Maybe she was seeking something deeper with God. Or maybe it was her subtle way of saying fuck you to the Church that had trapped her. I'll never know, but switching religions isn't something passive women do.

My mother watched her mother sacrifice everything with grace and learned that this was love, complete devotion, perfect restraint, never asking for more. When my mother became a mother, the pattern continued.

But I had choices she didn't. I could leave a bad marriage. I could have my own money. I could say no—to my husband, my family, even to her. I could choose my healing over everyone else's comfort.

The pattern of daughters becoming vessels for their mothers' unfinished pain stops here.

The Role They Gave Us

This pattern isn't unique to my family. Colonization created no-win situations for women like my grandmother. The census kept changing what race she was—mulatta in one decade, indio in the next. When everything about your identity is unstable, perfect behavior becomes essential.

What started as Georgina's way of staying safe became my mother's blueprint for how daughters should be. And that blueprint got passed down to me as anxiety, people-pleasing, and a deep belief that my worth depended on never making anyone uncomfortable.

I wasn't born this way. I inherited survival strategies from dangers that don't exist anymore.

Dr. Laura's Dichotomy

Before I had my daughters and learned how complicated motherhood would become, I worked as a graphic designer in a print shop in Hialeah, Florida. My office perched above a roaring Heidelberg printer, the smell of ink and press powder thick in the air. In the mid-nineties before podcasts or streaming, the only thing that cut through the mechanical thunder was an old silver radio, which was my lifeline to the outside world, crackling with Dr. Laura Schlessinger's call-in show.

I couldn't stand her conservative views, but when women called in to ask questions about their mothers, my mouse would freeze mid-design. I'd hold my breath, waiting for her answer, recognizing my own story in the women's pain.

One day, a caller shared about her mother in a way that mirrored my own relationship. Through the AM radio static and thundering press noise below me, Dr. Laura said something that stayed with me for decades:

"If she's lucky, a woman gets two chances to have a mother-daughter relationship. First, with her mother. And again, with her daughter."

Everything, and I mean everything, stopped. All I could hear was the press thirty feet below me and its predictable rhythm as it shot out piece after piece of my designs, stopping only when there was a problem with the color or when the enormous sheets of paper got jammed.

My office floor shook as it always had, and I sat there in front of my computer screen and started to cry.

That idea hit me hard. Because it suggested that it wasn't too late and that maybe I could still get this right, just not with my mother (obviously) but rather with a daughter of my own one day.

Maybe *I* could be the mother I needed. Maybe love between a mother and child could feel like love.

I understand now that healing doesn't work backward. You can't give what you never received until you first grieve what was taken. And what was taken from me began the night my brother died, not just losing him but also my right to be held in my own grief.

But even then, even with that fragile hope blooming in me, I hadn't yet stood in the truth of the original wound.

And that truth begins that night.

When Saving Her Became My Job

It was winter. I remember that. Cold in the way it got in the late eighties in Westchester County in late November. Brutal and piercing, as if the wind were punishing the tall evergreens on either side of my house for staying upright. I had just turned seventeen about six weeks before.

The knock came hard at 2:30 a.m. Insistent. It wasn't the kind of knock you could sleep through or pretend you hadn't heard. It rattled the house. I opened the door and there they were. A police officer. A priest. Two men standing like the grim messengers they were. Two blank cold faces.

They said his name.

My brother's name.

And that was all it took.

My mother stood behind me at the top of the stairs, still tying a knot in my father's thick burgundy robe that someone gave him to wear in the hospital before he died three years earlier. When she saw him, the priest, and heard David's name, she understood. And then, she screamed.

A sound ripped from her that I didn't know humans could make.

It wasn't just grief. It was their whole history. It was the blood from her placenta that had kept him warm and nourished and safe until he was born and for nineteen years after. It was a sound that came from deep inside the earth and burst out of her body. Erupting and boiling over, red-hot bloody embers flying and burning everything around her.

She collapsed.

Her hands clawed at the air. She dropped to the floor at the top of the stairs as if a bullet had shot straight through her heart.

I remained frozen at the doorway; my bare feet pressed flat into the cold slate tile my dad had laid down by hand a few years before. The chill stayed trapped at the soles of my feet like an ice pack. Above my ankles, the rest of my body went numb. My emotions turned off. No feelings were available to me. I focused on feeling the uneven ridges of the tile under my toes because it was the only thing I could actually feel. I thought about my dad, and his hands smoothing this grout. Did he ever imagine I'd be standing on his handiwork receiving news like this? I turned toward the messengers still standing shoulder to shoulder outside in the cold and could see my breath now and also their car in the driveway, headlights and emergency brake still on. My jaw in the gaping-open position for I don't know how long.

Death came right in through the front door that night and enveloped my mother.

And I disappeared. Not literally. But I did, from the inside.

Becoming Invisible

They didn't look at me. Or ask me if I was okay. The priest didn't speak to me as he made his way up the stairs. The police officer didn't meet my eyes after that first moment either. My mother never turned her head and I evaporated in the aftermath. A witness to a storm I was expected to help contain.

That moment taught me who I was allowed to be in a crisis, the one who absorbs. The one who doesn't break down. The one who becomes useful and stays good.

Daughters who learn their place become emotional shock absorbers for everyone else's pain. But who takes care of us? Who tends to our cracks?

That night set the precedent. From then on, her suffering took up all the oxygen in our house. My suffering, an afterthought. A luxury. Something I could return to later . . . if there was a later.

I didn't cry right away. I couldn't. I was holding her. Cleaning up. Notifying his friends. Holding space while no one held mine.

The water was rising in me, but I kept swallowing. That's what it felt like, carrying part of her grief so she wouldn't drown in it.

The Unspoken Vow

It felt like becoming a human container for all of her feelings, even when mine were flooding the room. It looked like translating her grief into daily tasks, into never missing a moment when she wanted to lock eyes with me and remember something together until we were both crying. I would never leave her hanging, but so often I felt that my energy was being siphoned off. Trauma bonding is what I think they call this now; it's insidious because after a while there's nothing left to connect to but darkness.

There are moments I remember like film stills.

Me standing in the doorway, her falling to her knees and screaming into the abyss.

The look on the priest's face like he'd never seen anguish and was barely keeping his shit together.

My hands trembling as I called my brother's friends one by one.

I remained calm and measured; they were falling apart on the other end of the calls, just like my mom.

The way the house sounded after—people walking in and out, that familiar sound of death, loss, and grief, just like when my dad died three years before.

I was underwater.

And in that stillness, I made a vow I didn't know I was making.

To be the one who didn't fall apart. To be strong for her because this is the worst thing that can happen to a parent. Everyone said this was much, much worse than losing a sibling and that I needed to be strong for her.

And I kept that vow. For years. Until the weight of it almost took me under.

We're never supposed to say that sometimes we hate our mothers. Not the women they could have been, but the mothers they actually were. We hate how they made us into their therapists, their emotional-support animals, their reason for living. We hate that loving them means abandoning ourselves. And we hate how even saying this feels like the worst thing we could do.

That night solidified my role as the one who holds it together and taught me that my grief was inconvenient. That good daughters swallow shock instead of feeling it. We learn that our role in family trauma isn't to heal, it's to step back so everyone else can fall apart safely.

It would take a long time to even begin to untether that night from my body. To understand how deeply I'd been shaped by her scream, by the way no one looked at me except to say I had to be strong, for her.

The way they convinced me that her pain was the *real pain*. The worthy pain. The only pain.

In Latino families, there's an unspoken hierarchy of suffering, and the mother's pain always comes first, second, and third. It's cultural and generational. They call it familismo—family above all else. But really, it's marianisimo. Mother above all else. Her pain, her sacrifice, her submission. That's the gold standard. Everything else is self-indulgent. Selfish. American.

This dynamic showed up everywhere. I was always the one who could handle more, who didn't need as much, who was "the strong one."[7] The data confirms what I felt—53 percent of Latinas report feeling pressure to support their family, but only 39 percent feel pressure to succeed in their careers.[8] We're literally sacrificing our dreams for family obligations[9] while believing this makes us virtuous.[10]

And maybe that's where it started, this tendency I have to carry more than I should. To go silent when I most need care. I think I may have built an entire part of my identity around not asking for anything. But I *do* know, at some point, I stopped expecting to be supported.

This pattern followed me everywhere, into every relationship, every job, every friendship. Always the one who could handle more, who didn't need as much, who was "*so* strong."[11] I wasn't just doing this in my personal life, I was doing it at work too. What researchers call "covering,"[12] modifying my communication style, my leadership approach, even my appearance, to fit white male standards, was just a professional extension of that same pattern. Despite asking for raises and promotions at the same rate as white men, only seventy-four Latinas get promoted to manager for every one hundred men.[13] Over a lifetime, this pattern costs us over $1 million in lost earnings.[14] I call it the Million Dollar Heist because we're literally sacrificing ourselves out of financial security while believing we're being good employees.

It's a mindset I adopted, as familiar as my mother's hands. Struggle equals virtue and pain equals worth. The more you sacrifice, the more deserving you become. In our culture, we wear our struggle like a badge of honor, proof that we're good daughters, good women, good mothers, good business owners, and good employees.

What do these kinds of beliefs do to a young girl? What does she become when her needs go untended for so long and when she doesn't have a clue how to tend to them herself?

We're doing it right now, together. Breaking that code and acknowledging these patterns out loud. Some might call you ungrateful, dramatic, too American. They might say you're betraying our culture, dishonoring your mother, forgetting where you came from. The isolation is brutal. Sometimes it feels easier to say nothing than to face a culture built on daughters who suffer without complaint. But keeping it all inside is killing us slowly. And somewhere in that killing, we're beginning to understand that our worthiness should not be dependent on how much pain we can withstand.

The Weight We Carry

In our culture, mothers are the only ones allowed to need and to take up space with their pain. Daughters are supposed to be grateful and available and invisible. Obedient mirrors for our mothers' expectations, never reflecting back our own.

Somewhere along the way, it became clear that support only came after collapse and that needing help was a privilege I had to earn through suffering.

I figured out the math pretty quickly. My problems only mattered if they were bigger disasters than hers, and asking for help was only okay when it didn't compete with her recovery. I became a professional crisis creator because it's the only language she understood. It was the only way to get her attention without being considered selfish. And when that becomes your baseline, your nervous system starts doing what it must to adapt.

It creates chaos.

Not because we're flawed. But because some part of you learns that you have to bleed to be seen.

I can see it now, how the whole pattern played out.

My crises weren't always visible. Sometimes it looked like pregnancy complications, like financial disarray, or staying in bad relationships way too long and not knowing when or how to get out.

And underneath I was a girl who was never allowed to make anything about herself. A girl whose grief was always less than someone else's. A girl who was expected to hold, but never to be held.

Even now, I hesitate to say it because I still carry the guilt, the shame, the voice that says, "You made this mess" and "This is *still* your fault."

For so long, I operated from this place of struggle. Every achievement had to be earned through suffering. Every bit of support had to be justified by a crisis. It was the language I learned to speak before I could speak English.

I'm trying to live into something different, and I want you to consider living into it as well because not everything that breaks around you is your doing.

Some of it was woven into us, some of it was modeled, and some of it was the residue of being told too many times that you were *too much*, or *not enough*, or simply *in the way.*

And, yes, you might be realizing that there are ways you reenacted a pattern. You see that now. You and me, we've created some messes, big and small, because some part of us believes that only in the aftermath are we allowed to be held.

The hardest part isn't seeing the pattern; it's accepting that breaking it might mean disappointing the very people who taught us that their disappointment was the worst thing that could happen to us. And maybe for the first time you can hear the loop playing over and over.

I know you don't want to live there anymore.

This isn't a clean ending. I don't have a perfect ribbon to tie around this.

But I *do* know you deserve love that arrives before you collapse and that you are worthy of care and support without having to first experience a major meltdown.

And if we can see the pattern, we can begin to end it. Maybe not perfectly, but honestly. With our eyes open. With our hearts open and with both feet on the ground.

This doesn't mean cutting our mothers out of our lives. It means cutting the cord that's been feeding them our life force. It means learning to love them as the flawed humans they are, not as the perfect mothers we needed them to be (or being the perfect daughter they expect).

I don't want us keeping our heads barely above water anymore.

I want us to live.

Maybe You Should Go Back to Therapy

The suggestion had come from a few different people over the months, but when it came from Emma, a client who'd become a trusted friend, I finally paid attention. Sometimes you need to hear something from the right person at the right moment.

My therapist, Cathy, was kind, but not soft. In our first session she asked what I wanted to get out of working together, and I told her I wanted peace. But what came instead was grief. Then rage. Old, heavy, unimaginable rage.

This anger wasn't just everyday frustration. This was what I'd always called "anger of the ages" when I described it to my husband—generational rage stored in my body, waking up and seeing a way out and wanting to be set free. I was so scared of its power, of what it might do if I really let it out.

Here I was, successful, working on a book, doing all the "right" things, and suddenly I was harboring this force that threatened to bulldoze everything I'd built. Like discovering you've been living with a dragon in your basement while hosting dinner parties upstairs.

Cathy didn't try to tame it or fix it or make it more palatable. She just witnessed it, she let it be what it was.

This was my first lesson in choosing triumph over struggle—that healing meant feeling everything fully, not pushing through it. The choice wasn't to avoid the pain, but to stop making it mean something was terribly wrong with me.

Later, I'd come to call this a "necessary struggle." The fury that felt so permanent, so threatening, ran its course because I finally allowed it to leave. I believed in its temporariness. The only reason it had felt permanent was because I wouldn't let myself fully feel it. By doing the hard work of feeling it completely, I softened and released it.

This was when I began to see it for what it was: The anger wasn't just mine. It belonged to my mother, my grandmother, generations of women who'd learned to alchemize their rage into resilience and their pain into productivity. And for the first time in decades, someone gave me space to feel it all.

As I began to untangle my personal relationship with struggle, I started recognizing how this pattern wasn't just mine. It was cultural, generational, and it had a saying we all knew by heart. Years earlier, I'd experienced this pattern in the most literal way possible.

Breaking the Chain

I named my daughter after Georgina not just because I wanted to honor my abuela's experience. I wanted to rewrite the legacy of motherhood for both of us. When I was pregnant with my Georgie, the doctors discovered something alarming: dangerously high blood pressure in the umbilical cord. A precursor to a condition called reverse flow (absent or reversed end diastolic flow or AREDF), where the natural order inverts and the baby begins feeding the mother. It's life-threatening. The very connection meant to sustain life becomes the thing that endangers it.

The threat loomed over us for a month before she was born. Every appointment, every ultrasound, watching for signs that the flow might reverse. My doctor was explicit that if it happened, my daughter would die if they couldn't deliver her in time.

I never imagined that years later I'd be watching for the same warning signs in my family patterns. And now, here I am. Awake. Watching this dangerous reversal in the patterns I didn't mean to pass down to my daughters. I haven't handed them the whole weight, but I've come dangerously close.

I see it in their reflexive apologies for simply needing something. In how they make themselves more convenient, less demanding, for no reason.

This is how trauma gets inherited by the daughters of strong, successful, high-functioning women. Not through the horrors we've survived, but through the things we never thought to question.

We exist in the liminal space between cultural worlds. Expected to be independent American women while experiencing the ever-present gravitational pull of our mothers' sacrifices. But we *can* evolve our way of mothering. We can honor our culture *and* love our children with boundaries, for them and for us.

The real taboo isn't that we shouldn't challenge our cultural traditions. It's that we shouldn't resent our mothers. And we're finally ready to say that part out loud.

That's where it begins. That's where it always begins.

I know this wasn't an easy chapter to read. It wasn't easy to write. But if you're still here, still believing, then you're ready to tell the truth about the roles you never asked for and the needs you've denied.

Repeat after me:

I am not broken for wanting safety.

I am not dramatic for needing support.

I am not selfish for grieving what I didn't get.

I am not ungrateful for wanting more than just getting by.

I am not disrespectful for questioning the traditions that hurt me and for working to build new ones that still honor my culture.

I am not "too American" for choosing to heal.

I am not responsible for healing my mother's childhood (or adulthood).

I am not required to be grateful for the bare minimum.

My worth isn't measured in how much I can tolerate, but in how deeply I can live.

Just as my pregnancy required constant monitoring for reverse flow, healing requires vigilant boundary setting. We must watch for signs that we're feeding others at the cost of our own life force. We must be ready to intervene, not with cruelty, but with the same medical urgency that saves lives.

Just as a body learns to protect itself after trauma, we learn to protect our spirit by choosing boundaries that honor who we are becoming. I want my daughters to grow up knowing they can deeply love their cultura while never sacrificing their own needs to prove that love.

I'm teaching them to honor their lineage while honoring themselves—to carry forward their heritage's beauty without carrying its burdens, to be proud Latinas who honor our traditions of resilience while creating new ones rooted in their own autonomy. This is how we begin to believe we are worthy, by treating our emotional well-being the same way doctors treat matters of survival. By understanding that some connections must be reimagined not out of hate or resentment, but out of love for life itself.

Worthiness was our birthright all along.

The pattern ends here and our healing begins now.

Breaking these patterns doesn't have to mean breaking family bonds. It does mean having the courage to say, "I can honor where I come from while forging a new path. I can cherish the beauty of my culture while releasing the burden of its unsustainable expectations."

I can love my mother and still choose to mother myself and my children differently.

She begins to believe she is worthy.

Reflection: Breaking the Chain While Keeping the Love

Hermana, I see you. I see you loving your familia so fiercely while silently carrying truths you've never been allowed to speak. I see you honoring the beautiful parts of our cultura—the way we show up for one another, the way love flows through every meal, every gathering, every sacrifice—while also feeling the weight of expectations that you were never meant to manage.

This reflection isn't about choosing between your culture and your healing; it's about creating space for both.

Take a moment with these questions. Not to judge yourself, but to finally give voice to what's been living in your heart.

1. What were you never allowed to say?
2. What truth are you carrying inside, still trying to talk yourself out of?
3. Is there a part of you that's still waiting to be rescued? What would happen if you knew you were enough to save yourself?

You don't have to lose that special kind of caring we have in our families to advocate for your own healing. You can keep the love while changing the pattern.

CHAPTER SEVEN

Don't Question the Culture, Part One:
Understanding Cultural Inheritance

The cultural programming we inherit isn't just about language or traditions; it's about invisible value systems that shape how we see ourselves and move through the world. Before we can reinvent anything, we have to understand what we're working with. This is the story of discovering the collision that's been controlling my life, and maybe yours too.

Before the shame found me, there was only joy.

My Latinidad wasn't something separate or set aside in my childhood; it was the soundtrack of our home and the rhythm we naturally moved to without thinking. My parents filled our house with music. Stored in the solid wooden shelves on the far side of our living room was a collection of instruments, such as Puerto Rican güiros, a cuatro, a classical guitar, and several sets of maracas, one with a hand-painted sunset at El Morro sealed beneath its glossy shell, the fort silhouetted with a Caribbean sky on fire. Instruments that weren't just decorative but indigenous to the island.

The güiros had two holes drilled out of them, just the right size for your thumb and middle finger. I used to press mine in and pretend I was playing even when no one was listening. One day I remember sticking a flashlight inside the hollow center, curious about what lived inside. It felt rough and coarse like it hadn't been meant to be touched. The outside was smooth and had what looked like a hundred perfectly parallel ridges about five inches wide and bunched together. When I dragged the metal fork against the ridges, the vibration started in my hand, then traveled up my jaw and buzzed in the back of my mouth. The sound was so soothing, and when I put my nose near the opening where your fingers go, I smelled something old and woody, carrying the history of a living thing that had died, been scooped out, and polished into something new. A gourd that wasn't meant to be eaten, but was still meant to feed us, just in a different way. The percussive sound is so distinct that, even now, hearing it brings me right back to my childhood living room.

My parents played records and sang along, busting out the instruments when family was over like it was the most natural thing in the world.

Spanish flowed through our conversations like water, mixing with English in that effortless dance I'd later learn to call Spanglish. "Mija, ven acá," my mom would call, then seamlessly switch to "Ayúdame in the kitchen." I practiced it the way kids practice anything, wanting to get better, never questioning whether I belonged to those sounds and syllables.

We celebrated everything. Three Kings' Day, weddings, birthdays, baby showers, graduations—there was always someone in our extended family accomplishing something worth honoring. My mom came from a large family, so cousins were constantly staying with us, or we were visiting them in Puerto Rico. I spent countless afternoons swimming in tropical beaches with my cousins, in kitchens eating food prepared by family members known for their signature dishes—"Prueba esto, mi amor, it's your titi's specialty"—or sitting in my grandmother's kitchen in Puerto Rico while she handed me a few hard shells from her almond tree.

I didn't know what they were, these unremarkable things that looked like a teardrop-shaped hard corkboard, smooth yet nothing special. My uncle took two in his hands, interlocked his fingers, and pressed them hard against each other until—*crack*. The pressure released the sweet white meat inside. Still one of my favorite flavors. It was a small magic trick: finding the softness inside something built to be impenetrable.

There was never any separation between "kid things" and "adult things." It was woven into the fabric of family life in Puerto Rico and at home in New York; it was normal to have extended conversations with my uncles, to learn from older cousins, to internalize the values that shaped how we moved through the world together. When my cousin Harry got engaged and needed to save money, it wasn't even a question—he moved from the island to live with us while he worked and saved. After my dad died, Harry naturally stepped in as the man of the house. Later when my cousin Robin got her master's at Columbia, she lived with my mom and stepfather. This wasn't unusual or seen as a burden, this is just how love works in our world. When family needs something, you make space. La comunidad se cuida. Taking care of each other is just what family does.

Eating food was a celebration, and joy was created out of the simplest things.

It was seamless. It was home. It was just who I was and who we were. I absolutely loved it.

What I treasure about our culture goes deeper than music or the food (okay, the food is pretty spectacular, but stay with me). It's the values woven into every interaction. The way we prioritize relationships over all. The belief that celebration isn't frivolous, it's how we honor our shared humanity. The understanding that you're never alone if you're connected to your people. This wasn't about what we did on holidays, it's how we actually lived.

My mom instilled in me one of her most powerful beliefs: *There's always a way*. And in her world, that way came through people, through her support system.

She knew that security isn't just about what you have; it's about whom you're in relationship with. This is how I understood resourcefulness, not as a hustle, but as an act of caring for a village that will care for you right back.

I watched my mom genuinely invest in the people around her. The community she was a part of always reciprocated. She never shared about it explicitly; I just watched it in action.

When I came to her with sketches of a prom dress I wanted to design, she got excited about supporting my dream of becoming a fashion designer. I was taking a sewing class in school and drawing designs in a sketchbook she'd gotten me, but there was no way I could actually make the dress myself.

My mom had a relationship with a seamstress—probably someone she'd helped along the way. She brought her my designs, we shopped for fabric together, and the seamstress made my prom dress by hand. Custom-made for my measurements and a fraction of what we would have paid at a store.

She was teaching me about community.

When I started screening my film across the country, something unexpected happened. The screenings came with invitations—dinners the night before, breakfast the morning of, late meals after. At those tables, with those people I felt the deepest level of cultural belonging I'd ever experienced. I'm lucky enough to have friends with whom I've felt a deep sense of connection for decades. But this cultural piece had always been missing, and when that space finally got filled, it felt like home. As if I were meeting long-lost primos out in the world that I didn't know I was related to—that familial recognition that goes a step beyond friendship.

I had given something to the community by making the film, and in return they reminded me how precious and essential it is to feel at home. That's when I decided to devote my work to teaching about belonging, because I knew that if I could help people create this connection, it could lead to lasting change.

But what made that sense of connection so meaningful was how unexpected it felt. Here I was, finally being embraced by the very community I'd spent my life believing that I'd disappointed.

This belief had deep roots in linguistic shame—that particular form of cultural trauma that comes from a thousand small cuts. Growing up hearing and feeling that my Spanish wasn't good enough taught me that communicating was dangerous. It wasn't teachers, they were always supportive. It wasn't even non-Latinos, whose opinions somehow didn't sting as much. It was family members and other Latinos who would respond with great disappointment when I struggled. "You need to learn how to speak better Spanish, Denise." Or the well-meaning comparisons: "Wow. If my family could speak another language, I'd do everything I could to learn it from them."

They never directly said, "Your Spanish isn't good enough." But with each comment, another drop of shame dripped into what would become a cavern as deep as the Grand Canyon.

I wasn't just afraid of speaking Spanish. I was afraid of speaking, period. When your language gets constantly criticized by the very people who were supposed to be your safe space, you learn that your voice itself is the problem. This warped into not understanding corporate speak, corporate rules, and the unspoken agreement that no one was going to be their true self in these spaces.

My last name didn't help—common in some Spanish-speaking countries but not here, and I mispronounced it too. Combined with my light skin, I had a recipe for easily hiding.

So many of us learn this dance early—María becomes Mary, Alejandra becomes Alex, Margarita becomes Maggie. We make ourselves easier to pronounce, easier to accept, easier to forget we were ever different at all.

That stubborn belief followed me everywhere, into job interviews, where I'd shrink myself without realizing it. I flew under the radar as much as possible. I didn't downplay my accomplishments, I forgot they existed entirely. I wasn't there to interview them; I was there begging to be accepted.

None of this was conscious. None of it felt like an actual choice I was making; it was more like a default setting. A familiar state of dissociation, that "trance of helplessness" I mentioned before.

This wasn't strategic self-preservation. It was something else entirely—my self-awareness so dull, I couldn't see that a choice existed.

It *was* a trance, but not a passive one. I didn't hide by making myself physically smaller; I hid by controlling my voltage. I regulated my breathing to be softer. I tamped down my natural enthusiasm until it fit into a professional-sized box. I learned that my raw passion read as unrefined, so I invented a version of myself that felt more acceptable. It wasn't that I felt inauthentic. I had become an expert at repackaging myself until the original version was unrecognizable.

I can't tell you how many people have shared similar stories with me—the gentleman who waited until the end of an event to confess he'd denied his whole Mexican identity to avoid language judgment, completely assimilating to look like a white guy. The tears that roll down faces when people admit they don't know the language their grandparents died speaking.

They put themselves in the back of the line, always ready to disappear. This is exactly how we show up professionally too. We take the seats farthest from decision-makers. We don't speak up in meetings until we're directly asked to. We volunteer for the work no one else wants rather than advocating for the projects that showcase our talents.

When you spend your life planning for escape, you never give yourself the chance to position yourself for leadership. We become excellent at being indispensable in roles that don't advance us, but invisible when it comes to the ones that do.

We don't negotiate salaries because asking feels risky. We don't apply for jobs unless we meet 110 percent of the qualifications. We stay in roles longer than we should because leaving feels like admitting we deserve better, and deserving better feels like we're tempting fate, like asking for too much when we should be grateful for anything at all. As if our ambition were a threat.

We are the common denominators in our own lives, and this shame doesn't stay personal; it has a professional price.

The saddest part is that this same belief crept into rooms full of Latinos I desperately wanted to be in—rooms with people who understood what it felt like to be the only one in predominantly white spaces, who knew the weight of code switching, who shared that particular brand of exhaustion of constantly translating yourself. Rooms where someone would mention where they bought ají dulce or culantro—those sofrito ingredients impossible to find outside New York and Miami (hint: your local Japanese grocery store—you're welcome)—and everyone would lean in with their own secret spots. Or where a reference to Selena or Bad Bunny would spark an instant connection.

But I'd panic at the thought of someone discovering I wasn't fully fluent in Spanish, or at family events where my Spanglish became everyone's favorite topic of conversation, or at speaking opportunities where I'd feel guilty about my success, specifically about how much money I was making, as if I didn't deserve it. This is where things get complicated for me, because for years something in me has always felt undeserving. I'd have to consciously go over my qualifications and accomplishments out loud so I could hear why someone would pay so much to hear me speak. Otherwise, and this is hard to write (but maybe you've felt this too), my default was that I was not worthy. Like this constant voice I couldn't turn off telling me I was failing some test I didn't even know I was taking.

It's as if there are two voices trying to sabotage us: one, from workplace racism, the microaggressions and unspoken pressure to abandon your collectivist values for individualistic ones that make you feel too different or like a "DEI hire." The other comes from cultural pressure to represent accurately, making you feel like you don't know enough about the culture to even call yourself Latino.

I'll admit, sometimes I catch myself judging people. Like when someone doesn't know a cultural reference I think they should, or when they seem less connected to the community than I think they ought to be. It's that split-second assessment, that measuring stick I didn't even know I was carrying.

We get treated as if we don't belong in workplaces. But then we judge each other even harder than outsiders do, as if our survival depends on an exclusionary standard of authenticity.

I saw this play out at a screening I did in Cambridge with mostly Harvard faculty, grad students, and a cohort of successful Latina Boston professionals. A student came up to me afterward and shared how a classmate from South America had been particularly unkind to her throughout their midcareer master's program at the Kennedy School. She'd always suspected it was because this student didn't think she was "Latina enough"—she was born in the United States.

There's this divide that cuts painfully deep when people born in Spanish-speaking countries sometimes treat those of us born in the diaspora as if we're not "real." After my screening, that same classmate approached her and apologized. "I didn't realize what I was doing when I was judging you like that," she said. "I am not going to do that anymore."

We've been carrying this fear that if we don't gatekeep our own culture, it will disappear, and the numbers seem to support that theory. Spanish use at home among US-born Latinos has dropped from about 67 percent in 1980 to 55 percent in 2021, according to Pew Research.[1] But I don't think people are consciously thinking this through when they judge. It's not as rational as "Hey, we're losing our language, so you need to learn it." It's more existential than that.

When I moved to Miami, I made a phone call, probably to a doctor's office or something routine, and mispronounced my last name. I'd been saying "SO-ler" my whole life, even though it's "so-LEHR." We were the Soler family at church in Spanish Harlem and in the Bronx when we were visiting family and friends and of course when we were in Puerto Rico. But when we moved to Westchester, my parents anglicized the pronunciation.

The receptionist gave me an earful: "¡Ay, no! ¡Tu apellido es So-LEHR, no SO-ler! Si no lo pronuncias bien, es el principio del fin de nuestra cultura. Esto es algo pequeño, pero es algo muy grande. Tienes que estar orgullosa de donde vienes, y pronunciar tu nombre correctamente demuestra que estás orgullosa."

And you know what? From that point on, I always pronounced it correctly. Our cultural legacy *does* matter. And to this day I'm grateful she called me out—I do the same in my own way now. When I meet someone who's anglicized their name or mispronounces it, I gently share this story. I don't let it slide. I can see the pride return immediately. They stand a bit straighter as they reclaim this part of themselves.

We get messages every day that we don't belong. From politicians. From the daily television news, and films that ignore our substantial role at the box office. From educators and colleagues who mispronounce our names and somehow make us feel that we should apologize for the inconvenience.

But the most painful rejections come from inside our own community.

I Assumed His Name Was Carlos

I met Charles when we hired him to design our first website for Project Eñye. We were in the development phase of the film and were producing these short digital stories for YouTube, exploring identity and belonging in the Latino community. Little did I know he'd become one of our most powerful stories himself, another voice from that in-between space I knew so well.

When I first saw his name on the proposal, I assumed it was

Americanized from Carlos. I was miffed. Then I caught myself in that same judgmental space I'd felt from others (because apparently, we all do this crap) and immediately went to *I need to know this guy's story.* Because for sure somebody that looked like him, that called himself Charles, had a good story.

Turns out his actual birth name was Charles. Not Roberto going by Robert, or Jesús going by Jay, stories I'd heard so many times before. Just Charles. Son of a Salvadoran mother and white father who met while he was in the Peace Corps. The marriage didn't last and Charles grew up with his father in the Pacific Northwest, as far from his mother's culture as you could get while still being on the same continent.

He looked puro Latino. Dark skin, with features that echoed his Salvadoran roots. But his story kept revealing layers of this same theme of not measuring up, not belonging, not being "Latino enough." Yet another casualty of the collective expectations around what makes someone "authentic."

That was his daily reality, looking like the culture that kept rejecting him. Spanish speakers would greet him with familiar warmth, assuming a shared language, shared experience. But when he couldn't reply, their faces would change. That subtle shift from welcoming to withdrawal. The same judgment I knew all too well, reflected in Charles's eyes.

How dare he not be able to speak Spanish.

Hearing about how the community had turned cold on Charles, I realized something that cut deep. We who knew the sting of being "othered" had become expert gatekeepers ourselves. We'd become the colonizers of our own people, drawing lines between "real" and "not real enough" with surgical precision.

What does a "real" Latino even look like anyway? Is it in the melanin in our skin? The passport stamps? The fluency or accent we speak Spanish with? The rhythm in our hips? The way we say or spell Mami or bendición or coño? The cultural longing? My friend Irene Vilar describes the first-gen experience as a "nostalgia for a place we were never born." The perpetual grief of feeling ever so slightly outside the circle.

The conquistadors are long gone, but their playbook survived. And without realizing it, we've learned to use it against each other.

How many times have we been the ones shifting our face from warm to cold? From welcoming someone to judging them? How often have we asked someone (directly or silently) to prove they belong?

And we don't just draw those lines in language. We draw them in skin tone, hair texture, features, where they were born or came of age and educated. Let's be honest, Afro-Latinos have been erased from this conversation for decades. They show up in our communities, our families, our history books (if we're lucky enough to have any), and still get treated like outsiders. As if Blackness disqualifies a person from their Latinidad. As if you have to choose one identity over the other, and whichever you choose, someone will tell you that you got it wrong.

I don't share this from a place of having lived that reality; I haven't. But I've seen what erasure does. I've seen it in rooms where Afro-Latinos are present, but not included. And if I'm here to tell the truth about belonging, I can't stay silent about who has been left out.

Charles's face alone made him a target for these expectations. The more Indigenous his features, the heavier the burden of cultural authenticity he was expected to carry. It wasn't just about language anymore; it was about who has the right to claim their own identity and who appoints themselves the judge of it.

In our interview, he described what happened when people saw him: "What breaks the spell is the minute that people see me, they start engaging with me in Spanish and I can't talk back. And it's a very frustrating thing. It's frustrating for two reasons. One, I'm a little disappointed in myself that I can't talk back, so I feel like I'm letting myself down a little bit. And then the other thing is the look on the faces of the people engaging me are like, 'Why don't you know Spanish? You look like you should.'"

His story broke something open in our community. After his interview aired, others started reaching out. They'd been carrying these secrets, these shameful admissions of not feeling "Latino enough," believing they were alone. But in seeing his face, hearing his story, they recognized themselves.

I didn't expect sharing his story would transform Charles himself, but something was unlocked when he found a safe space to share his truth. The story gave him permission to choose himself first. And from that place of self-acceptance, he could finally reach toward the culture that had always been his birthright.

The stories kept coming after Charles's interview aired—not just a few, but from droves of people who felt exactly as he did. At every screening, every keynote, they'd find me. A young Colombian woman adopted by white parents in Denver. A first-gen Guatemalan young man who was part of the catering crew at a Boston event, who waited in that line of secrets and dreams to tell me he felt that it wasn't an accident he was working that night so he could hear my message. A Mexican gentleman in the Bay Area who shared that he'd actually lied and told people he wasn't Mexican, ashamed because he couldn't speak Spanish. Different circumstances, same wound, and the constant pressure on people to prove they belonged in their own skin.

Each story that came to me in my inbox, after screenings, in intimate conversations, showed me how deep this goes. We're not just hurting individuals—we're creating a generation of people who feel like strangers in their own culture. But questioning these standards feels like dismantling something vital, so we classify it under "preserving la cultura" and keep turning away from one of the most heartbreaking rejections of our own people.

I know what it's like to be bullied, four years of hell I shared in my film. I remember doing whatever I could to avoid them. Changed my route to class, never used their favorite bathroom, hunkered my shoulders down and got as small as I could as I walked past them in the crowded high school hallways. The same thing happens with cultural rejection. People would rather peel themselves away from their ancestry than expose themselves one more time to this painful dismissal. I've seen it firsthand, all over the country. They shared the shame with me in confidence; a secret they've never told anyone.

Watching Charles reclaim his story taught me our power isn't in the in-between space itself; it's in our choice to stop letting others weaponize it against us. To stop waiting for permission from the very people who've made us feel unwelcome and to embrace our complicated, messy cultural identity on our own terms, not anyone else's.

I think about him now, and how sharing his story gave him permission to stop waiting for approval and start claiming his birthright. But even watching his reclamation, I was still caught in my own pattern of compensation, still feeling that I had to earn my worthiness instead of simply existing in my own skin.

The dissonance was becoming unbearable. I could help others find their way to belonging, but I was still knocking on that same door, still trying to prove I deserved to enter a world I was born into.

This judgment lives in thousands of Latino bodies. We carry that weight on our shoulders, in our throats, and throughout our nervous systems. It's this constant fear that at any moment we could fail an arbitrary unwritten cultural test.

This doesn't just mess with us. It gets passed down, and I'm tired of handing it to the next generation.

Something had to break. And it was about to.

Where Shame Found Me

The basement of the Church of the Good Neighbor in Spanish Harlem had that church-basement smell—the residue of decades of celebrations and sorrows, First Communions and funerals, wedding receptions and memorial services. This was where we spent every Sunday without fail, where my parents had gotten married, where my grandmother worshipped, where my uncle had been pastor, and where my aunt led the choir. I'd spent countless hours playing in the sun of its small courtyard while the adults talked inside.

I was always excited to see my mom's friends because they were always so excited to see me—the same delight I experience now when I see the children of my closest friends grow, reminding me of how much history there is between us, how much love, and the power of relationships that stand the test of time. These friends had slept over at our house, staying up late singing Beatles songs and Spanish church hymns like "De colores." Many of them were in my parents' wedding pictures, each one so loving and curious and expressive toward me.

This room held generations of our family's story, and I felt like I was part of it all.

Like so many Latino spaces, church was where we learned to navigate between how we felt and how we were expected to show up.

I was five when shame first found me there.

Just a year into our Westchester life, we'd moved from a two-bedroom apartment in the Bronx where all five of us had been squeezed together, where my brother had gotten the same bike stolen twice, where the neighborhood was changing for the worse, to a four-bedroom house on an acre of land in one of the wealthiest counties in America. Tall evergreens on both sides and an acre of thick woods behind the house. I'd later learn my parents could barely afford it, but they were determined to give us opportunities they never had. It couldn't have looked, sounded, or smelled more different. We were the only Latino family in the entire school.

I was still holding my mother's hand as we passed through the downstairs hallway of the church, the fellowship room opening ahead of us, sunlight streaming in from the cement courtyard. The open doors invited fresh air and the bustling sounds of the city into the room. Car horns, distant music, voices calling to each other, all mixing with animated Spanish conversations as people caught up after the service. It created a familiar soundtrack that felt like home.

One of my mom's friends spotted us and took a few steps our way to say hello. Spanish weaved through the space between them like an invisible thread I couldn't quite grasp.

Then she turned to me, crouching down to my five-year-old eye level, grabbing my hand.

"Hola, Denise." She had a thick accent and smiled. "Remember me?"

I didn't.

"¿Hablas español?"

I confessed, "Un poquito." The universal response of every kid who's been caught culturally red-handed.

"¿No puedes hablar español?"

Her smile fell off her face. Like gravity suddenly agreed with her disappointment, pulling every joyful muscle down in a split second. Her body shot up like an accordion being stretched way out. The confusion in her voice when she said: "¡Ay, Lolin! ¡No me digas! ¿Ella no puede hablar español?"

The heat hit the back of my neck like invisible rays of painfully hot sunshine were beating down on me. The pelitos at my hairline stood up in rigid attention. My shoulders went weak, an early lesson in how my body responds to shame. I couldn't move. Heart beating like it would pop a hole through my chest. I was so mad at myself for something I had no control over. I couldn't look at her, so I looked at the floor, my eyes finding safety in the nonsensical stringy gray waves in the vinyl floor. I stared at the wavy thickness of those lines that led nowhere because trying to decipher the artist's logic felt safer than watching my mother struggle to defend my deficit. It was the first time I saw her make excuses for me, but it wouldn't be the last. I grabbed her hand and squeezed as I looked up at her, but she was deep in the back-and-forth of being scolded and defending herself. I hunched over and held my breath.

They went on to discuss my inability to speak Spanish as if it were a modern-day tragedy. I was a human cautionary tale right there in the church basement. A living example of what happens when you let your children drift too far from their roots.

In that instant, I made a decision about the world and myself: I was a disappointment, and it wasn't safe to be who I was in my cultural world because my very existence was a letdown.

I wondered if on that day when my parents celebrated their marriage, in that very space, if my father had already decided not to teach his children Spanish. I'm so curious to understand why he made that decision and what had happened in his life to make him so firm on his position.

I have theories about his choice. His father was Cuban, his mother, an orphan from Puerto Rico, and he grew up in 1950s New York City during a time when Puerto Ricans were arriving in large numbers after Operation Bootstrap. Many white Americans reacted by calling them lazy, loud, or uneducated, racist stereotypes tied to colonial attitudes. Cubans faced similar biases. My father grew up between worlds, not fully embraced by white America and maybe not feeling fully embraced elsewhere either. The safest move was to blend in and teach your kids English only.

The irony is that both my parents' decisions came from the same place—wanting us to belong. My father believed belonging meant perfect English and full assimilation. My mother believed belonging meant staying connected to our culture through language.

My relationship with Spanish has been complicated ever since. I've tried to reclaim it over the years—private tutors, Rosetta Stone, Duolingo, online live group classes, countless starts and stops. On my very best days, I'm fluent like a fifth grader. I joke that the more glasses of pinot grigio I have, the more fluent I get.

It's always felt like holding something precious in the palm of my open hand; it's there, but it's never quite secure in my grasp.

That pain didn't stay mine for long; it became a bridge. My imperfect Spanish made me relatable to others who were denied the language as kids. The language gap became both my scar and my superpower, proof that belonging doesn't require perfection.

On the road with the film, I'd met thousands of first gens with the same story of parents who chose not to teach their kids Spanish. Some were completely in the dark, as I was, about why their parents made that choice, and others understood what was behind the decision: necessity. Do I think we would have been better off learning Spanish as children? Absolutely. I see how much pain the not knowing causes, how our own community uses language as the number one way to exclude someone and tell them they don't belong, how easily this group gets shamed. I value Spanish so much that I sent my daughters to a private international school—not just for the hours of exposure each week, but so bilingualism would be the norm, not the exception.

But I also believe it should not be the defining factor of our Latinidad. Learning a language as an adult—try learning Mandarin or Portuguese at thirty, for example—is vastly different from the ease of learning as a child. And trying to learn it while carrying deep shame until you're fluent is an especially cruel burden.

The values my family passed down to me are precious: a relentless work ethic; family loyalty; resourcefulness; and the belief that there's always a way through every problem. These values, including the ability to find joy and play music even in hard times, shaped who I am and how I'm raising my daughters.

But some of the collective wisdom of my parents' generation worked against my generation's individual needs, even as it tried to serve us. I was taught to give and give until I was exhausted, but never how to set boundaries at work or advocate for myself. To work hard but not how to "play the game." I was never even warned that there was one, let alone how difficult it would be to navigate. Overgiving is so valued in our culture that I brought familismo to my professional life, thinking *that* was the game—I'd say yes to everything, help as many people as I could. I'd work endless hours, believing that's how you proved your value.

The Spanish decision was another example of this pattern, loving protection that sometimes limited what was possible for us.

Here's what I figured out later: When kids don't feel emotionally safe, they develop a kind of hypervigilance. Not because they're in physical danger, but because emotional disconnection can feel like a threat. So, our brilliant nervous systems learn to read every single tone shift and micro-expression. I've always been obsessed with body language—I could detect someone's discomfort before it exploded, predict what people were feeling before they said a word. And I softened myself accordingly.

This whole thing wasn't just about not speaking the language. It was about existing in that liminal space even inside myself, learning to manage by becoming incredibly tuned in to everyone else's internal world while completely suppressing my own.

It took me years to realize I'd built my entire identity around this. I didn't know who I was if I wasn't fixing, translating, buffering, or shrinking for other people.

This all came to a head when I decided to make the film. For seventeen years, I didn't think I was the right person to make it. Surely there was somebody more qualified than me who could tell this story. Out of all the obstacles—the money that needed to be secured, having no filmmaking skills, no connections—the one thing that kept me from moving forward for seventeen years wasn't any of that. It was that I couldn't speak Spanish fluently. That's the reason I didn't think I would be the right person to tell this story.

I didn't even recognize it myself. I disregarded my own perceptiveness, treating it like a side skill useful in coaching, maybe, but not something I could lead with. I minimized it, tucked it away, played small with it. Like being a virtuoso pianist but only ever playing to an audience of one. My attunement wasn't abstract; it was how I read the room.

In corporate environments, I muffled my wisdom completely. The more I tried to play that corporate game, the less I could hear the truth of my inner voice. Pain has a way of sharpening perception. When you have the capacity to experience grief and shame, you're able to feel that with others and recognize yourself in them. But in professional settings, I had a hard time with that discernment. I shut it off because it was so hard to understand what was going on amid all the lack of authenticity.

I came alive when I started working on the film. That's where I felt like I could shine. While interviewing over a hundred people, I was able to access this part of me in conversations that were deeply meaningful.

I remember sitting across from them, mid-interview, watching their eyes well up. They weren't even crying yet, but I could feel the heavy emotion in my own chest. So many shared, "I've never told anyone that before." And I wanted to say, "Me neither." That moment should've felt like proof that I was doing something right. Instead, I felt that I was getting away with something I wasn't supposed to be good at.

There was this fulcrum moment—I can't tell you how many interviews it took—when I realized that I am not the only one who feels tension around our cultural identity. And knowing that to my core dissolved walls between me and other people.

That's when I started trusting my intuition. I felt free to share what came to mind, whereas before I might have censored it. I realized with great certainty that nothing separates me from another human being. *When I feel separate, it's because I've forgotten.* When I feel that connection and trust that truth, I have full access to my instincts and my confidence. That's why making the film and doing interviews felt like magic to me, not like work. Work felt like a place I had to put up walls and constrict my personality. But through the film, this book, my coaching, and speaking, the more I trusted the truth that we're not separate from one another, the more authentic I became. Because if we both know pain, we don't need walls between us. There's just that authentic understanding between human beings.

That should have been the clue. The tell. The hidden cost of the early shame. I couldn't fully embrace the gift I'd developed because of it.

From Wound to Gift

I've discovered my gift is authentic presence, and I can't turn it on or off. When I'm fully present without any pretenses, I'm often able to get to the heart of a matter. In one-on-one coaching conversations, I can usually see the issue. Onstage, I can feel what the audience needs, whether it's one person or thousands.

My film, *being eñye*, explored the "ni de aquí, ni de allá" experience, and in the process, I unintentionally created a movement around helping people caught between worlds find belonging.

I crafted talks, led workshops, stood on stages, and watched faces light up with recognition. "I thought I was alone"—the phrase I've heard most in the last ten years. Our most personal struggles are often our deepest collective wounds.

I can sense what people try to hide, that perpetual not-enoughness, the exhaustion of existing between worlds, the fear of being alone in all of it. For years I thought this ability was only valuable if it helped others. I was wrong.

This gift doesn't need to serve anyone else to be worthy. It's valuable because it's mine. I learned that I am worthy not because of what I do, but because I exist.

I started to see the impossibility of quantifying "enough." Poked holes in that whole construct. The faces of people who dealt with the same circumstances became my own healing—when I feel that not-enoughness creep in now, I can quickly recognize the lie for what it is.

I felt the loneliness of individuals caught between worlds: Latinos, LGBTQ folks, trans people, anyone stuck in the liminality of two identities. My favorite conversations were those that helped them understand: You're normal. You're not alone. And that middle space where you exist is real. You can create something entirely new. A hybrid identity that's individual, custom, completely your own design.

On corporate stages, I shared stories most people would never tell publicly, modeling what it looks like to sit inside a messy, imperfect truth. People would say, "I wish I could be that courageous." Those conversations started to loosen the rules. What does "professional" really mean? Who's watching? Whose approval do you actually need? And we discussed the radical idea that you're entitled to comfort, that you don't have to code-switch your way through everything.

But because this gift emerged from that early wound of feeling imperfect, I dismissed it. Treated it like an adaptive strategy rather than the strength it had become. I couldn't claim it as my own because I resented the origin.

It became the most fulfilling work I've ever done. Still is. My heart in all of this is to help people feel less alone, because when people feel truly connected, as if they're an integral and important part of their communities, workplaces, and families, that's when belonging can thrive.

But here's what I want you to know: Underneath all that rubble of shame, shape-shifting, and cultural confusion, there's something magical that belongs only to you. Your bicultural brain is brilliant. And this sometimes messy in-between space where you live is where your most powerful insights come from.

Over time, I saw this pattern repeat, again and again. But what I really learned is that every woman I worked with had her own unique gift buried under years of believing she wasn't enough. The soft-spoken one had profound wisdom. The "too loud" one had infectious leadership energy. The perfectionist had incredible attention to detail that could transform entire teams.

Your gift is there too. It's not despite your cultural experience, it's because of it. The question isn't whether you're worthy. The question is what magic have you been hiding under all that trying to fit in?

The Gift of Familia in Corporate Spaces

I'll never forget that prom dress, or the lesson embedded in how it came to be.

Years later, when my film started getting attention, I began receiving the most interesting emails. People would contact me wanting to bring me to screen the film and speak at their company, but they weren't in leadership roles to make that decision. We're talking about some of the biggest, most recognizable brands in the world.

They used that distinctly Latino resourcefulness, working through employee resource groups (ERGs) or informal groups they'd cultivated, and somehow made it happen. They got me there, paid my fee, and screened my film.

There it was as clear as day; this was the same resourcefulness I'd watched my mother use. They used the same knowing she had that there was always someone whom she knew, who might know somebody else who could help. They used the same confidence in our community's willingness and ability to make things happen.

These weren't executives or event planners, they were support staff, assistants, interns, people without traditional authority. But together, they created opportunities that seemed otherwise impossible on paper. They navigated corporate bureaucracies and found resources in ways that would make an MBA program jealous. This adaptive intelligence—the knowing my mother taught me, that there's always a way—was creating real business results in Fortune 500 companies.

But here's what made them even more extraordinary: They created events around the events. Meet and greets, lunches, dinners before and after. Opportunities for me to meet and get to know their bosses, their coworkers, and sometimes even their parents and their children. These events felt as if I were meeting cousins I'd just never met before. There were layers of relationships, care, and celebration that went far beyond the professional. They deepened their relationships with one another and with me.

It was so different from how I'd later get hired through traditional channels—event organizers who would book me, tell me what time to be there for sound check, and that was it.

For these Latino professionals, it was about nurturing familia. They were doing this at the biggest companies you can imagine and somehow making corporate spaces feel like family gatherings.

In Latino culture, you don't lead with your accomplishments. You let people discover who you are through relationships, through how you treat others, through your actions. Humility isn't just politeness, it's a core value about recognizing everyone's inherent worth, and it's a hell of a way to treat people.

Respect is given without question, to elders, to people who've lived through things, to anyone who shows up with good intentions, to people of authority. We don't make people prove themselves before they're worthy of basic human dignity.

But in American business culture, if you don't announce your credentials, people assume you don't have any. Respect must be earned through what you've achieved, not who you are as a human. You're supposed to lead with your résumé, your wins, your value proposition.

I've spent years caught between these two approaches.

People constantly tell me I'm too humble, that I don't "play myself up" enough. I can easily spot when the women I coach miss opportunities to claim their expertise, but when it comes to doing the same for myself, I struggle so hard to overcome the internal resistance.

It's not that I don't know my worth. It's that leading with accomplishments feels like violating something sacred about how we're supposed to treat one another.

This humility, this resistance to claiming space, it doesn't exist in a vacuum. It's connected to something much deeper, something that affects our entire community.

Language is a place where we learned to police ourselves and each other.

The Bigger Picture

Not speaking Spanish as a Latino is one of our culture's deepest taboos. It's not just frowned upon; it's treated as a moral failing, a betrayal of identity itself.

We're mad at the wrong people.

Instead of judging who's "real enough," we should be asking why we're keeping score at all. How we've become gatekeepers of our own culture, turning away our own people, the ones who could help it thrive and evolve and fortify it for future generations.

We get furious at awards shows when our talents aren't recognized, at entire industries that turn their backs on us, but tell me again: Who's a real Latino?

I knew my own pain around this. What I didn't know was how many others carried this same wound, or how deep and damaging it is.

Instead of fighting to fit in, we need to make the definition of "fitting in" way bigger. It's about recognizing that sometimes the most powerful contributions come from those of us who live in the spaces in between, who can see both sides because we've never fully belonged to either.

That church-basement moment wasn't just my story. Years later, I'd meet countless others carrying the same wound, each of us thinking we were alone in our shame. Charles was one of them. His story would break something open in our community, revealing how these individual moments of shame connect to a larger pattern of cultural gatekeeping that affects us all. The shame shows up differently for each of us. For some, it's about language. For others, it's about success itself.

Maria and the Invisible Collision

I met Maria early in my journey. She was the CMO of a major TV network, and she'd reached out after seeing our first few stories on YouTube. Her email was . . . well, let's just say I read it about twenty times. Here was this powerful media executive gushing about our work, about how we were the only ones telling the stories of the most influential generation of Latinos—the first gens. The ones born here, trying to navigate two worlds with no road map.

We flew out to LA for a business meeting, and Maria invited us to her home while we were there. That's when she dropped something on me that would change everything.

"The value system Latinos are steeped in," she told me, "it's called collectivism. We prioritize the family, the group, the community. And that collides head-on with how you succeed in American workplaces, through individualism."

Maria Lopez Twena (formerly Lopez Knowles), whose groundbreaking Duality Framework research at Entravision documented this cultural collision extensively,[2] was putting words to something I'd felt my entire career but never understood.

Boom. The light bulb finally went on.

Suddenly, every story I'd collected, every workplace struggle I'd witnessed, including my own constant need to prove my worth at work, made all kinds of sense. I wasn't failing at my career; instead I was caught between two diametrically opposed value systems, trying to succeed in one while being wired to win in the other.

The group-first mentality is like the scaffolding of our diaspora experience. You can't see it, but it holds everything together. It explains why we prioritize family over everything. Why we live with our parents longer than our American friends have the ability to understand. Why we give endless respect to the older generation. Why asking for help outside the family feels like airing dirty laundry. Why being successful can feel like abandoning our families. Why we guard secrets like precious jewels and keep our shame to ourselves. It's why that church-basement moment had such power to bring the whole structure down.

Meanwhile, the United States runs on individualism. Everything here centers the self. Independence. Personal achievement. Setting boundaries with family. Taking credit for your work. The American dream, baby!

The exact opposite of everything we've been taught to value.

Understanding this clash didn't just explain why I was struggling;

it showed me why so many of us feel like failures in both worlds. We're not doing it wrong. We're trying to win a game and the rules we know are the opposite of the ones we *need* to know.

So imagine what happens when a Latina walks into her boss's office to ask for a raise. She's operating under collectivist values, proudly sharing what her team achieved together. But corporate America runs on individualism, where winning means taking individual credit and promoting ourselves and self-advocating. Oh! And don't take anything personally because "it's just business."

The Latina in this story does not get the raise, but you probably already knew that.

Why? Because she wasn't taught to emphasize her value over the team's. She can't bring herself to say, "I delivered this project," because it feels like ignoring the hard work from everyone on her team, every person who in some way contributed to the whole. Meanwhile, her colleague down the hall is getting promoted for work that was actually a team effort—but he had no problem taking the credit.

The statistics back this up in devastating detail. Latinas earn just fifty-five cents for every dollar paid to white men[3]—the big heist, and it's happening right under our noses.

I lived this for years. In countless meetings I should have taken credit for my contributions, but instead I'd deflect, "It was a team effort." The credit went nowhere or, worse, someone else eventually claimed it. In performance reviews I never once said "I." It was always "we accomplished," "we delivered," "we exceeded goals." It never occurred to me that I was supposed to advocate for myself.

And I wasn't alone. Working with Latino ERGs across different industries, I heard the same phrase over and over: "My work speaks for itself." It was so common that I had to stop people midsentence and say, "No, your work is not going to speak for itself, *you* have to speak for your work." We take pride in how hard we work, how much we give, how we never complain. I wonder how many of us are overworking and overgiving right now waiting for someone to eventually notice our dedication.

The discomfort was real when self-promotion came up. "It just doesn't feel authentic," people would tell me. "I don't want to pretend that other people weren't involved in the process. It feels weird to take the credit, wrong even." This is the professional expression of that foundational belief I explored earlier in the book, los trapos sucios se lavan en casa. Subscribing to this belief contributes to our reluctance to discuss workplace challenges and demand better treatment.

The discomfort made sense. The pressure I was seeing reflected the same workplace dynamics I'd researched earlier—that constant demand to conform to individualistic values that feel completely foreign to how we were shaped.

Even within our own community this collision plays out. In our early days, someone on my team reached out to a Latino speaker whose name kept coming up in corporate ERG circles. She approached him with collectivist values: Let's collaborate, share opportunities, lift each other up. He declined, sharing that it didn't make sense to him to help his competition. Pure individualism. It showed me how the system rewards individualism so effectively that even within our own community some have fully embraced the "competition over collaboration" mentality.

On a more positive note, I was fascinated to learn that Latino ERG groups became little bastions of collectivism within individualistic corporations, safe spaces where crediting the team was valued, where thinking about one another was respected rather than questioned. But step outside that bubble and we're back to clawing our way to the top, where promotion disparities show just how steep that climb really is.

Individualism doesn't 100 percent compute for us. It feels inauthentic because, to us, it is.

So we end up caught in the impossible bind, failing at American self-reliance while simultaneously betraying Latino collectivism.

The guilt is ever constant. Wanting more than what our parents sacrificed to provide. Feeling guilty if we go to therapy (or just want to) when they "handled their problems alone." Setting boundaries when they gave everything to our family.

Finally understanding this explained so much. It explained why I felt like such a disappointment to my family. Why my independence was seen as rejection. Why asking questions made me seem disrespectful. Why going on vacation anywhere but home was seen as "selfish." Why my grief was only acceptable if it served someone else. Why choosing myself was seen as betraying the whole. It explained every moment of judgment, every disapproving look, every subtle shift from welcome to withdrawal, from that church basement to Charles's story to countless others I would go on to hear.

Understanding this didn't make the pain magically disappear. But it certainly helped me stop carrying all that shame. It helped me see that I wasn't deficient or lacking. I was just built differently from the values I was being measured against.

And once I understood this, my work was never the same. Because the real story isn't about language or culture or even belonging. It's not about choosing sides or holding two worlds in balance.

It's about having the guts to stand right in the middle of two opposing sides and decide, "I'm not picking." To create a space entirely our own, where we can define ourselves on our own terms.

She sees the collision clearly.

CHAPTER EIGHT

Don't Question the Culture, Part Two:

Reinventing Ourselves on Our Own Terms

Once you see the collision clearly, you have a choice: keep getting crushed between two worlds, or create something entirely new. This is the story of choosing the harder path, reinventing myself on my own terms instead of waiting for permission to belong as I am. Maybe you're ready to make that choice too.

How to Fight Power, the Need for Permission, and Machismo in Real Time

I was brought in as a consultant for a local ad agency whose client had finally realized that simply translating their campaigns into Spanish wasn't enough to reach the Latino market. They needed someone who understood the nuances, the cultural shifts happening between generations. Someone who could see and understand what others couldn't.

And I delivered. The campaign we created was built on deep cultural intelligence about Latino values—not language. In a workshop I'd delivered to their team, I'd taught them about the "we" culture versus the "I" culture, about honoring family connections, multigenerational living, the importance of genuine invitations rather than empty pleasantries. How humility runs so deep that self-advocacy feels foreign, that work ethic and integrity matter more than flashy promises, that honoring those who came before us is sacred. We took those values and went deep, crafting a campaign specifically for first-generation women, those born here with at least one parent from a Spanish-speaking country. This is my sweet spot: first-gen Latinas born in the USA. Our target was the mom juggling cultural expectations, and the younger single woman navigating her own path. We included thoughtful touches of Spanglish that spoke directly to these women, so they'd know this campaign was designed for them. It was such an uncommon message, and I was so proud to help deliver it.

The team seemed surprised and a bit relieved at how accurate my insights were about this market. I'd produced an entire film about this demographic, interviewed over one hundred people for both the movie and my podcast, and I'm part of the demographic myself. By that time, I'd been on the road for six years doing about fifty engagements a year, having thousands of conversations with people who wanted to share their stories with me after screenings and keynotes. I understood the qualitative insights deeply.

But my expertise still sounded foreign to them—no pun intended. So they went looking for evidence to substantiate what I was telling them. I had mixed feelings when they came back saying they'd found research to back up everything I'd said. It was the most respected research available, the Duality Framework,[1] created by Maria Lopez Twena, my mentor, under the umbrella of Entravision Communications, the media company where she'd worked as the CMO. Yes, of course I was right. But it bugged me that they'd felt the need to verify my professional (and lived) expertise in the first place.

How many of us have been in rooms where our qualifications are questioned, where teams of people feel comfortable fact-checking our credibility in ways they'd never do to others? Where being highly credentialed somehow still isn't enough, where our knowledge gets treated as suspicious until validated by external sources? It's the tax we pay for existing in spaces that weren't designed for us—having to prove over and over that we belong, that we know what we're talking about, that our perspective and authority have value.

After the campaign was up and running, I received a call that a board member on the client's side was concerned about the campaign. He disagreed with the tactic of speaking English to attract Latinos and was "disappointed" with the execution. The agency called to fill me in and to ask if I'd be willing to jump on a call with him to support the strategy. I wasn't happy about what I'd be walking into, but I accepted the invitation because I felt so strongly about the work and stood behind it 100 percent. Plus, my reputation was on the line.

I was asked to get on the call fifteen minutes before to "strategize," which is when they told me how the call would go. They shared that they'd take the reins and that I would be in a supportive role, only speaking if I was asked something directly. The president of the agency and the account executive would do most of the talking. The client was on the call as well and would be taking more of an active role. I agreed, and all four of us talked about how great the campaign was already doing. The client mentioned it had surpassed their goals and we weren't even at the halfway mark.

Then the board member showed up on the call.

The call opened with everyone introducing themselves, and of course the board member went first. He launched into his qualifications with the rapid-fire confidence of someone who'd perfected this spiel, his voice deep and overpowering. It was the vocal equivalent of a man on a crowded subway splaying his legs wide, energetically elbowing everyone else to make room for his ego. He rattled through his leadership titles, his board appointments, how many years he'd lived here, casually dropping that he also kept a place in Mexico, each accomplishment delivered with practiced speed while sticking the landing on the points he knew would impress. His voice oozed that particular brand of machismo we know all too well, aggressive energy that makes you want to step back and protect your space. Ay, por favor, we've all met this guy. When he's not sure he belongs, he bulldozes the room to prove he does. He tried to claim every inch of conversational real estate, but all I could think was how exhaustingly predictable his whole intro was.

He showed no curiosity about my perspective. Instead, he expressed shock that a campaign targeting Latinos wasn't in Spanish and questioned my experience, my approach, my understanding of "our people." But he had it completely wrong. He thought this campaign was directed toward immigrants and primary Spanish speakers. It wasn't. This was for first-generation Americans whose first language is English, who speak in Spanglish and navigate the world through a sophisticated blend of cultural values that he couldn't even see.

"See, Denise, we come from two different generations. You don't understand how we think," he said, his voice dripping with condescension.

He had my bio. He'd seen my accomplishments. But none of that mattered because he was the board member, and everyone else on the call treated him by default like the expert. The agency president who'd promised to "take the reins"? Silent. The account executive who'd praised my insights in internal meetings? Also silent. But this wasn't just quiet, it was selective muteness. Looking at their faces on the screen, I saw what was really happening. They weren't just staying quiet, they were watching an accident they had orchestrated. It felt like I was in a professional free fall, the ground dropping out from under me while they looked on from the safety of the ledge. My body went rigid. I was the sacrificial lamb, thrown under the bus to save the account. They left me to defend work that had already exceeded the client's goals, against a man who fundamentally misunderstood the target audience, their faces tight with the tension of watching me burn alone.

Five people were on that call, but only he and I knew what we were really discussing. Everyone else disappeared. The client remained silent about how well the campaign was going despite the board member's disagreement with the execution.

"I want to know whose idea it was to speak Spanglish in the ads? It's so unsophisticated."

When I explained we were targeting the children of immigrants born here who primarily speak English, he went silent. "No one told me that," he said. No apology. Just a wall. The call ended with his paternalistic platitudes about what this generation should know and do, and no resolution on the campaign.

That's when I finally felt the true weight of my isolation. Not just my physical aloneness on that call, but the deeper isolation that comes from standing in that space between worlds, between expectations, between ways of being, and finding no one there standing with you.

Because when people you assume are your community throw you under the bus, where do you belong?

When the gringos who employed you don't have your back either. Deference was given to him because he was the board member, leaving me in the role of having to prove my worthiness.

If I had had the data on hand, I would have taken a deep breath and with a smile, clearly and calmly, shared the same metrics of the campaign that the client had loved: Hotel-room bookings had well exceeded their goals for where we were in the campaign and we weren't even halfway through the scheduled run.

So, what do you do when you find yourself in a similar moment? When the board member realized he was in the wrong about the target audience, I had a small window of opportunity to establish my expertise with this market and I took it.

I shared my receipts—all of them. I'd coproduced and codirected a film about first-generation Latinos, interviewing over one hundred people, I had an award-winning podcast, and Apple had recognized me as a Featured Host. I was working on a book proposal specifically about the Latino community. I'd spent years on the road and had met countless Latinos who'd shared their lived experiences with me after screenings. I had a deeper qualitative understanding of this audience than most researchers—my road-tested experience validated what their data revealed. I mentioned that *NBC Nightly News* had brought me on as their culture expert for a segment called "Are You Latino If You Don't Speak Spanish?" After which I explained why Spanglish was the right approach for this demographic.

Mujer, when you know your stuff, lead with your expertise.

Don't wait for permission (or an invitation) to share what you know. Have all your credentials ready, your experience documented, and your confidence intact. The room needs to hear *you* are the expert—*so tell them.*

Here's how being the "diverse voice" actually works in corporate spaces: You're valuable until you're inconvenient. You're "insightful" until you challenge the power structure. You're authentic until you dare to exist in complexity. And when they abandon you, you're supposed to be grateful they invited you to the table in the first place.

The irony doesn't escape me, how we can be both colonizer and colonized in the same moment. This man, using his power to shame another Latino. The client, choosing distance over solidarity. Me, bringing my education and expertise to help corporations better "reach" my own people. All of us caught in this dance between belonging and betrayal.

Colonization doesn't just live in history books. It lives in conference calls when allies stay silent because it's "business." It lives in how sometimes we become what we fought against, making each other feel less than for existing between worlds.

Here's how I've learned to set boundaries with colonists, machistas, and cultural gatekeepers who try to stand in our way:

Before a meeting, substantiate everything. I mean, become masterful at documenting. Have your credentials, your data, your success stories ready. Know your worth in numbers they understand. In the moment, do not let any interruptions slide. Say, "I wasn't finished" (or just keep talking—this actually works!). When machistas at work (and in life) try to take up too much space, be ready to cut them off, interrupt, disconnect, and question them right back. Don't let your credentials get undermined without pushing back. And when you do get challenged, don't hesitate to answer with power and confidence. Be specific and firm. "Actually, I've spent six years researching this demographic."

Do not let condescension pass. When colonizers project their expectations and prejudices on you, hold up the mirror and request that they explain what they mean. Keep breathing, remain calm and professional, pero put them in their place: "That's an interesting assumption. Here's what the data actually shows." When the meeting is done, follow up in writing: "Per our conversation, I want to clarify . . ." Capture the facts, their behavior, what was said, todo. Create a paper trail, your future self will thank you.

The hardest part is that sometimes you have to pick your battles. But *never* choose their comfort over your dignity. And when they abandon you, remember, their table was never worthy of you anyway.

Understanding and Claiming Your Own Power

I won't pretend it's easy. I won't pretend it's simple. But living between two cultures, and understanding our values, *is* a profound advantage. You can live an enriched, authentic, and successful life on your own terms. You just have to do the work to articulate and claim what's yours.

And that matters because when you stop trying to fit someone else's definition, when you stop asking for permission, you begin to see the power of the in-between.

I used to think I had to choose, between languages, between family and self, between the pieces I was given and the parts I never felt worthy to claim.

But we were never meant to fit into one world. We stand in contradictions and make something new. Not because it's comfortable, but because that's where we already are.

This is how we reinvent ourselves. We stop trying to earn belonging and start choosing to belong to ourselves.

I was leading a coaching call for a small group of Latina entrepreneurs in a program designed to explore how cultural beliefs affect our ability to make money and lead successfully. We'd been exploring familismo, that deep loyalty to family that can sometimes keep us small. I'd been deep in my book edits, wrestling with my own "good girl" programming, when something profound happened.

I decided to pose a question that had been floating around in my head and asked them to fill in the blank to this statement:

"A good Latina daughter in my family would never __________."

I wasn't prepared for what happened next. The energy of the Zoom call transformed immediately. As the first woman spoke, something magical began to happen. What followed felt sacred and completely different from the cowardly silence of the corporate boardroom.

I sat straight up in my office chair, my body reacting before my brain could. Waves of electricity ran down my legs—"thigh chills" I call them—my body's unmistakable signal that I'm hearing something profoundly true. It felt like we were all floating above the ordinary world. Like we'd tapped into some kind of ancient brujería that was making anything feel possible. As if by calling out these old rules we were casting the spell that could break them. These women were filling the silence with their raw truth, and for the first time, we were liberating ourselves from the most powerful belief of them all, that devotion to family means sacrificing ourselves.

One by one, these accomplished women, entrepreneurs, podcasters, community leaders, revealed unlivable contradictions they'd been navigating:

A good Latina daughter in my family . . .

". . . would never stop talking to her mother . . . even when that relationship is toxic."

". . . would never leave a stable job to follow her dreams . . . even when she's sitting on a million-dollar idea."

". . . would never not have children . . . even when she's created a sense of familia for an entire community."

"... would never get divorced ... even after twenty years of shrinking herself to fit someone else's idea of who she should be."

"... would never move away from home ... even when staying means giving up the life she's always dreamed of."

As I listened to each woman, I realized we were all carrying the same invisible programming, like background music we'd stopped hearing but that was still controlling our choices. These beliefs work exactly like city sounds.

When we lived in downtown Denver, our apartment was constantly filled with white noise—police sirens, buses rumbling past, fire trucks blaring through intersections, people shouting in the alleys at all hours. We'd adapted completely and didn't notice any of it. But when friends would visit, they'd say, "How can you sleep with all this noise?" We didn't hear a thing.

That's exactly how these cultural beliefs work. The song of "You know you're not a good girl because ..." plays constantly in the background, not only making us feel like crap and that we're never enough, but also guiding every decision we make, what we accept, what we think we deserve, how we show up in relationships in our personal lives and at work. And we have no clue this is what's happening.

Our standards are low and we don't know why. We accept less money than we're worth. We stay in relationships that drain us. We shrink ourselves in meetings. We apologize for taking up space—the results speak for themselves. We are dissatisfied somewhere and have no clue it's because this song has us believing all kinds of lies about who we're allowed to be and what we're allowed to want.

And it's been playing so damn long we can't even hear it anymore.

We only start recognizing that song is playing because things *aren't working.*

We're not making the money we want. We're in relationships we don't like, jobs we're no longer happy in. We realize we've settled for something we're not willing to accept anymore. Something triggers the whole thing, and that's when we start to hear the music that's been controlling our lives.

We needed to change the record. And I walked everyone through a process that works at the neurological level:

First, recognize what song is playing. Think of something that's really bugging you. Be honest, this is just for you. Are you not happy in your job? Your relationship? Are you sick of something that you've been ignoring? Write that down now. What are you just tired of?

Now answer this question:

What would a good Latina in your family never do?

Answer like this:

"A good Latina in my family would never . . ."

Note: It's okay if what you want to write or what you wrote is upsetting. Actually, it's an indication that you've spoken the truth.

Here's where it gets powerful: Now flip it. What would a good Latina do—*on your terms?*

"A good Latina would . . ."

Maybe it's:

"A good Latina would make time to dance and sing by herself to loud Latin music of her choice for at least ten minutes a day—*no cleaning required!*"

"A good Latina would prioritize her mental health over keeping everyone else comfortable—even if that means not attending a family obligation."

"A good Latina would cook beans—black, pinto, kidney, refried, whatever—that bring her joy without worrying about the bean-authenticity police!"

"A good Latina would create sacred rituals that honor her culture in her own way."

"A good Latina would charge what she's worth (or negotiate an appropriate salary) without apologizing for knowing her value."

Now take a second to connect that thing you just wrote and the thing you're upset about at work, in a relationship, wherever it's showing up. If you need to, go for a walk or take a shower. Invite your mind to make a connection. When you see it, you'll understand how deeply it has shaped your life.

Then I want you to focus on what it has cost you to believe this lie. Because you know it's not true. It's just what you believed when you didn't have any business making a decision about what to believe about life, otherwise known as your childhood. No one has ever changed the music, but you are about to, and that is going to help you change everything.

The next step is to consciously switch out the record. I had them visualize walking to a record player and putting on a new record—taking off the old one and putting on a new one. This isn't just metaphor; this is how we create new neural pathways.

Finally, choose your new song. Redefine what a "good Latina" means on your own terms. Create your declaration, your new melody that honors your cultura while also honoring *you*. What does a good Latina look like when she's free to be herself?

Maybe she makes her abuela's recipes exactly, or maybe she puts her own twist on them. Maybe she lives next door to her familia, or maybe she loves them fiercely from across the country. Maybe she has ten kids or maybe she mothers an entire community in other ways.

Write down your new lyrics. What would a good Latina do when she no longer feels she needs anyone's approval? When she gets to define goodness for herself while still claiming every vibrant part of her heritage?

This is *your* cultura reimagined. This is your new song.

What makes this actually work is consciously practicing it over and over. Every time you catch that old pattern playing, you visualize changing the record. Do this enough times and, slowly, you'll begin to feel less stuck and more free.

This is what's called moving from conscious competence to unconscious competence. At first, you have to think about it—"catch" the old belief and consciously switch to the new one. But eventually, through practice, it becomes automatic. You notice the old song, change the record, and often feel better. That's when you know you're changing the underlying belief.

The shift was immediate and real. Women who'd been apologizing for their success started claiming their power. The entrepreneur finally saw herself as a "steward of her gifts." The community leader recognized she'd already created the familia she thought she was missing. The woman going through divorce stopped calling herself inadequate and started seeing herself as a phoenix rising.

This wasn't about rejecting our culture or abandoning our values. This was about consciously choosing which values serve us and which ones keep us trapped.

Here's the other side of changing the record . . . sometimes you need to switch off the other's song too. When your boss expects you to work 24/7, you get to say, "I deliver excellent work during business hours."

When they push individualistic competition over collaboration, you get to model a different way: "I believe we're stronger when we work together." When they want you to put career over familia, you get to redefine success: "My family commitments make me a better leader, not a less committed one."

The key is knowing which of our values are actually superpowers in disguise. Collectivism is called "team building" in corporate speak, and *you* are naturally good at it. Relationship focus is referred to as "emotional intelligence," and it's what makes great leaders. The instinct to take care of your familia is called "work-life integration," and it's what sustainable success looks like.

So, when they try to play the songs that make you feel that you have to choose between achievement and authenticity, you get to change the record too. You get to show them that there's a better way to work, to lead, and to succeed. And when you do it con ganas and you have results to back it up, you're not just changing your life, you're changing the entire "workplace culture," which is what they call it when Latinas start running things.

This is what reinvention actually looks like. Not some dramatic life overhaul or complete personality transformation. It's a decision followed by a metric ton of small actions—literally becoming the DJ of your own life, switching out the song you used to play for the one you choose to play.

Every time that old soundtrack kicks in, "Good Latina girls don't do this, good Latina daughters never do that," you get to say, "Nope, changing the record." And you consciously choose your new song instead.

The reason this feels so unsustainable isn't because we're defective or because we're failing at being "good Latinas." It's because we've been conditioned to play it safe and yet we push the limits anyway.

We are not broken. We are designed to push back.

Think about it. If these cultural expectations truly fit who we were meant to be, *why would following them feel so painful?* Why would shrinking ourselves create such deep resentment? Why would we keep bumping up against these invisible barriers if we were meant to stay within them?

The discomfort in your body is your signal, and the restlessness is your compass. That voice in your head saying, "This isn't right for me," is the validation.

We get to be the DJ of our own lives. Start by asking yourself, What would a good Latina in my family never do? Then change the record and ask yourself, What would a good Latina do when she gets to define goodness for herself?

She reinvents herself on her own terms.

Reflection: Songs for Your Future Self

We get to be the DJ of our own lives. Every time that old programming kicks in—"Good girls don't do this, good daughters never do that"—you get to say, "Nope, changing the record." And you consciously choose your new song instead.

Here's your first assignment as the DJ of your own life:

Create a playlist that makes you feel like the woman you're becoming. Songs that make you want to run, dance, celebrate, move. Music that sounds like freedom, like power, like the future version of yourself who's already figured this out.

She's not some distant dream. She's you.

CHAPTER NINE

Beyond la Lucha:

How to Choose Triumph After Struggle

You know that moment when your body knows something your mind hasn't figured out yet? Mine happened in a Safeway parking lot.

I'm standing twenty steps behind my car, frozen in place while my daughters and husband wait inside, groceries already loaded. They're probably wondering why I can't seem to move. But I can't. My feet feel like they're hot glued to the sticky asphalt. Because in this ordinary moment, under the mile-high Denver suburban sky, everything I thought I knew about strength, about worthiness, about what it means to thrive as a Latina in this world is starting to come undone.

A message that finally made sense of why I'd gone back to therapy years earlier—why healing keeps revealing new layers of truth.

But to understand how a routine grocery store trip turned into a moment of liberation, we need to go back earlier that day. Back to the library, where I'd spent hours doing what I call "time traveling"—diving deep into my past to excavate stories for the book I've been writing for years.

This wasn't pleasant work. Every time I sat down at my computer, old wounds demanded to be remembered. Experiences I'd done such a good job forgetting over a lifetime forced their way through my fingers and onto the page. Into the light. Pain I didn't want to feel anymore insisted on being described in excruciating detail. All this surfacing of the past was preparing me for a moment of clarity that would change my approach to unlearning and healing forever. Standing in that grocery store parking lot, I finally understood the pattern that had been running my life.

Most days it left me disoriented, like a computer processing in the background while trying to function normally in the foreground.

On this particular day, the memories hit harder than usual. I wasn't sure why at first. But when things start to feel especially hard and when despair creeps in around the edges, my mind goes to the same place it always has . . .

My brother.

Not just the devastation of losing him. But the way the community responded to that loss. The way they told me, at seventeen, to be strong. Not for myself, for my mother. I never realized, until writing this book, how deeply their suggestions shaped me, how not feeling like I had space to grieve became one of my earliest lessons in self-erasure.

There wasn't time or space for my pain back then. And gradually, I decided it was easier, and maybe even more honorable, to keep choosing to be strong over allowing myself to feel deep sorrow.

And it became a habit.

And here I was again, in the Safeway parking lot, groceries in the car, my family waiting, and I could feel myself doing it again. Slipping back into that familiar inner story: "You don't get to feel this. You just have to push through."

But then something else surfaced.

A memory I hadn't thought about in years.

When my brother died, I missed him so much it was hard to breathe. His charisma. His warmth. His ability to make everyone feel seen. He was magnetic. People loved him. And I loved who I was around him, playful, unguarded, and endlessly silly. When he died, I felt like that part of me died too.

But on one especially hard day of missing him, I remembered something I'd heard years earlier at a Debbie Ford seminar, something that didn't make full sense to me at the time, but stayed with me anyway.

"The universe is holographic. Everything is part of the whole. And the whole is accessible from any one part."

In my heart, I knew what I needed to do. What I loved in him, I could embody in me. So, I started showing up with more warmth. More humor. More love for people. Not to become him. But to keep the best parts of him alive through me.

That was a triumph. Not one anyone could visibly see, but one I had chosen and needed to remember.

That day, I almost chose grief as my identity. Instead, I remembered who I really am. And what I'm capable of choosing now.

But that parking lot revelation didn't happen in isolation. It was the culmination of months of writing this book, of excavating my past and sitting with memories I'd buried so deep I'd forgotten they were there.

And, as I dug through decades of carefully buried experiences, a devastating pattern emerged that I couldn't ignore. I was attached to struggle. Addicted to it, even.

I couldn't experience something beautiful without simultaneously bracing for something terrible. There was always something I was suffering for, always some catastrophe happening or lurking just around the corner.

The revelation devastated me. This wasn't the relieving kind of "aha moment" that lifts weight from our shoulders. This one made me sad. And it made me crave homemade Rice Krispies treats and the healing power of my daughters' laughter to tether me back to what was real.

Earlier, as I picked my kids up from their last day of school, my mind, craving sweetness and distraction, was still churning.

How could I have seen things this way? How did I become so addicted to this pattern?

Standing there in that parking lot, I finally understood this behavior that had ruled my life for decades. It was like the purest part of my soul finally recognized itself beneath all the inherited stories, like coming home to who I'd always been before the world taught me I needed to suffer to belong.

Daily Choice

MORNING: What would I choose today if I believed I was already worthy?

MIDDAY: Am I making something harder than it needs to be?

EVENING: Where did I choose ease today? Where did I choose struggle?

If you're reading this and it sounds familiar, and if struggle feels like your native language, your invisible badge of honor, I want you to hear this: You didn't invent this. It was passed down to you from women who were taught the same thing—that love meant sacrifice. That rest was lazy and joy could be dangerous.

But the pattern can stop with you.

That day in the parking lot, I realized that liberation doesn't always look like a revolution. Sometimes it looks like just deciding that you don't have to do it this way anymore and trying to figure out how.

Actually, changing the pattern required help I'd been too proud to ask for, and understanding where it all came from in the first place.

La Lucha Sigue

"La lucha sigue" is a phrase we know by heart. It's been passed down through generations, shared and shouted and carried in the marrow of our families. The saying isn't just about *personal* struggle, it's about *collective* perseverance, and the fight for justice, and dignity, and legacy. I honor that. We need that.

But somewhere along the way, I internalized it not just as a political or collective call, but as a personal code. I attached my worth to how much I could endure. I came to believe that struggle was the price I had to pay for every good thing. That, sure, things were going great, but also, if I wasn't suffering somewhere in my life, I wasn't doing it right.

Maybe this is your story too. Generations of sacrifice became the foundation for how you think success works. Our parents and grandparents really did have to struggle, mightily, just to survive. Crossing borders, working multiple jobs, facing discrimination, sending money they could have used for their own well-being home.

Layer on top of that our Catholic roots, which codify pain as the pathway to true redemption. Even if you've left the Church or switched denominations, like my grandmother Georgina did, these stories feel like permanent parts of our POV. A trauma trifecta: survival, sacrifice, and sanctified suffering.

In those Zoom sessions with my therapist, Cathy, I unleashed the kind of anger I didn't know I was allowed to feel. She never flinched. And something about that, about bearing witness, made me start to question everything I knew about what struggle was supposed to look like. What if all this time I'd been choosing a path I never had to walk?

Breaking free from intergenerational patterns isn't like flipping a switch. It's a process of healing soul wounds that have been passed down through lifetimes by finally saying, "This stops with me." But first, I had to understand what "this" actually was.

In our community, our ancestors' pain is sacred, and our ease is suspect. When you've carried generations of deprivation, of institutional racism, of having to fight for every inch of ground, anything that comes too easily feels untrustworthy, and struggle (unfortunately) feels comforting and familiar. It's like a kind of cultural Stockholm syndrome and choosing the devil you know over the uncertainty of something better.

But it wasn't just la lucha I'd grown up with. It was an entire constellation of family secrets and cultural taboos designed to keep us looking unbreakable from the outside, no matter what was crumbling within.

The taboo against admitting you're not okay. The secret shame of needing help. The unspoken rule that successful people don't struggle, with anything, and if they do, they certainly don't talk about it. The unwritten commandment that airing your problems is a betrayal of family loyalty.

These weren't conscious lessons. No one sat me down and said, "Mija, remember to suffer gracefully." They were transmitted through the unsaid, what wasn't shared, what was carefully edited out of every family story.

Some truths were so explosive they had to be buried alive.

The Hijacking of a Battle Cry

But how did we get here? How did one of our most powerful declarations of resistance become a trap?

La lucha sigue was born from movements that demanded fundamental human dignity. César Chávez and Dolores Huerta used it to rally farmworkers against exploitation. It echoed through the Chicano Movement, the East Los Angeles Blowouts, and every fight for civil rights and justice. In its original form, the fight was external, systemic, and shared. The phrase meant "*We* haven't achieved justice yet, so *we* keep fighting together."

The lucha was always supposed to be collective. But we, the daughters of la lucha, inherited something different—we learned to carry the fight alone.

But something shifted when the nature of our battles changed. It happened when the work moved from massive, visible collective actions such as strikes, protests, and legislative battles to the individual navigation of corporate ladders, academic systems, and professional spaces.

When we're the only one in rooms that weren't made for people like us, we start thinking it's our fault when things are hard. What should be everyone's problem becomes our personal shame. The story gets twisted and becomes "You have to make it on your own to prove your family's sacrifices mattered."

The never-give-up attitude that kept our ancestors alive became the only way our families knew how to teach us to succeed.

Add to that the belief that hardship makes you a good person, that having it easy means you're doing something wrong, that you have to earn happiness through pain first. If you're not suffering, you must not be trying hard enough.

So la lucha sigue, which was supposed to inspire us to fight injustice together, was reduced to suffering alone in solitude. The most powerful rallying cry in our history slowly became a chain around our own freedom.

Once I unpacked it, I thought I'd put it behind me. But life has a way of testing if you've really learned the lesson.

How to Come Back from a Fall

When the political climate shifted, my speaking work dried up almost overnight.

Within six months, I lost $75,000 in speaking business.

Over the course of a year, that $75,000 had become $200,000 in lost speaking revenue because of the current administration's rollbacks and budget cuts on DEI initiatives. Accounts were being closed. Opportunities that had become my professional identity vanished. We couldn't keep up with our daughter's dance classes and eventually pulled her out of the company altogether—devastating for parents who preach following your dreams. We were one month away from losing everything, and we had no backup plan. None.

I was panicking. Deeply ashamed. I gave myself zero grace. No space to grieve, recalibrate, or even breathe. I felt shame for not pivoting faster; the writing had been on the wall for months.

For someone who had built her entire career on being visible, on speaking truth to power, I suddenly had no frame of reference for where I was professionally. So, I did what I always did when life got overwhelming.

I contracted. I made myself smaller. I questioned everything. I buried my light because shining it felt too risky in a world that suddenly seemed hostile to everything I represented.

This was my old pattern talking, the one I'd been carrying since childhood. The one that reminded me, when things get scary, disappear. The chill of it felt familiar, almost comforting in its predictability.

There it was again. When life got scary, I pulled back. It didn't matter that I was a successful speaker with a book deal. Shame doesn't give a damn about your accomplishments. The pattern was playing out again, just as it had my whole life. Fear drove the bus, and I was half asleep, choosing the discomfort I knew over the change that I feared.

But my body had other plans.

The last two months in my old house were brutal. My speaking business was bleeding out, and I had built nothing solid underneath it. No foundation or safety net. A painful sebaceous cyst started growing on the back of my right shoulder. It had happened twice before, always during stress storms, but I'd ignored the pattern. Just as I ignored the one forming in my bank account.

Week by week, the cyst grew. So did the pressure. Money was tight, and I refused to spend a dime on a doctor. I kept the cyst clean and told myself I'd be fine. That was my coping mechanism, the one I'd learned as a child: endure, control, survive. Carry the weight no matter how much it hurts.

Still, something in me knew I had to start showing up for myself. I listened to the voice I usually brushed off, the one that gently nudged me out of bed at 6:00 a.m. Before the house stirred, before the emails started, I was out the door. This was about resetting my, at the time, very off rhythm. Right foot, left foot, inhale, exhale. The sound of my thrift store sneakers on the pavement became a metronome, organizing a mind that felt chaotic, anchored by the pull of Cookie, my very enthusiastic Labrador mix who was thrilled about our new ritual. The cold morning air didn't bother me at all because I knew I'd warm up. The walk felt like it was scrubbing the mess out of my life and I found my way back to me again.

They became a sacred promise I kept to myself.

If the day went sideways . . .

If I lost another gig . . .

If everything felt like it was falling apart . . .

At least I didn't bail on me.

That morning walk became my ritual. My reset.

For the first time in decades, I wasn't trying to disappear. I wasn't making myself smaller or dulling my light. I was just . . . present and available. In my body. In my life. It was the beginning of remembering that it wasn't necessary to hide to feel safe.

All while that bulge on my shoulder throbbed, growing into a painful, golf-ball-size mound. I was carrying the weight of everything I couldn't control, everything I thought I had to endure alone. For two full months, I held it together while preparing to leave the house I never loved, for the neighborhood I'd been dreaming of for twenty years.

Then, just a few days before the move, after a hot shower, it burst.

I'll spare you the full visual, but it was messy. Bloody, pus-filled, and agonizing. The pain radiated six inches in every direction. I wouldn't let anyone near that side of my body. Over the next few days, the cyst continued to leak and ooze, as if my body were finally releasing everything I'd been holding that was never mine to carry in the first place.

I took it as a sign.

The pressure that had been building was finally releasing. The hard part was behind me. I could sense something new was coming.

But first, we had to get through moving week.

We were packing up six years of life. Six years of ignored corners, too many plastic bins, and at least five boxes I'd never unpacked from the last move. I was sweating through another sleepless night, knee-deep in cardboard, bubble wrap, and all kinds of regret. My mind looped nonstop:

Why is this happening?

What if we can't afford the move?

What if I never rebuild my business?

Why didn't I pivot sooner?

What if, what if, what if . . .

Then something shifted. Like a major switch flipped.

I paused. Looked around at the chaos, and suddenly I knew.

I did this.

Every last box. Every overdue decision. Every ignored instinct. Which meant . . . I could change it.

In that moment, I took radical responsibility.

Not the bullshit self-shaming kind, but the kind that actually frees you.

I decided that if I'd created this reality, I could also uncreate it. I could build something better. Something aligned. I felt tapped into something divine. As if I'd finally remembered who I was.

And from that place, I heard it clear as day . . . *There's nothing bigger than me.*

Not the trauma that taught me beauty was dangerous. Not the

shame that made me hide my light or the fear that kept me small. Not the invisible backpack I'd been carrying for decades. I was bigger than all of it. And for the first time, I believed it.

I fully surrendered. I stopped fighting the fall and began to feel myself come back.

What would happen if you believed that about yourself? That there's nothing—no trauma, no pattern, no fear, no weight you've been holding that's bigger than your power to transform it?

By the time we moved into our small garden-level apartment on the edge of Wash Park—Washington Park, Denver's version of ocean-front property—the cyst was almost completely gone. A small scar remained. Evidence and a necessary reminder of my power to heal.

The apartment was a third of the size of our house. The ceilings were lower, the closets nonexistent. We had a minor spider problem and much to my daughter's chagrin, a loud cricket lived and sang loudly behind our fridge the first week we lived there. Though it kept them up at night, I didn't mind the noise. Because I felt lighter, freer, and happier.

Lighter. That's the word. For the first time in my life, I understood what it felt like to move through the world without that crushing weight on my back.

After ten months of free-falling, I wasn't falling apart anymore; I was coming together.

I wasn't a victim, I wasn't cursed, and I no longer felt stuck.

I was bigger than all of it.

I connected to the God version of me. My sacred center. The voice that speaks only truth.

We all have that part. The one we can trust. The one that took me forever to trust and the one that kept whispering to me every morning for years, "Get up and walk, Denise."

Not for weight loss or productivity, but because I needed an anchor to ground me in no longer abandoning myself. Because keeping a promise to myself was a radical act of self-love.

This is a full departure from how I used to live. I'm tuning in now. To me. Instead of carrying everyone else's expectations and fears, I'm trusting my own. I was raised to consider how *others* felt, so for years I missed every signal my body tried to tell me.

Now I know what "yes" feels like. I know what "no" feels like. And I still live by that rule I made for myself: When I feel "I don't know," I treat it as a "no for now."

When I listen, things flow. When I don't, I feel it immediately, and I remind myself: *You already know. You've always known. Tap into that knowing.*

And so, I do what she says. I listen to her and I move with the kind of trust I used to reserve for everyone else.

From Revelations to Liberation

Before I left that parking lot, I said these words out loud:

"I forgive myself for believing pain was a requirement."

This wasn't just about breaking a cycle. It was about reimagining what strength could look like. True power lies not in our capacity to endure suffering, but in our courage to choose differently. To say yes to joy, to rest, to rebuilding without first having to break.

Now, when my daughters rage, when they stomp their feet or scream their frustrations or let their anger fill a room, I don't rush to shut them down. I don't tell them to turn down their intensity, to be good girls, or to find the silver lining. Instead, I witness them, just as Cathy witnessed me. I let them know that their anger is valid, that it doesn't make them bad or wrong or unworthy. That they don't have to transform it into something more palatable to be loved.

When I look at my daughters, I see more than just the next generation. I see the possibility of a new way forward, one that includes softness, where success doesn't require their sacrifice, and where joy doesn't need to be fought for. Maybe that's the real revolution, not just surviving la lucha, but daring to transform it.

The Weight We Carry

Imagine someone strapped a backpack to your five-year-old body and, while wagging their pointer finger, said, "You wear this every day or you're worthless. This is how we'll know you deserve to exist."

And you believed them because you were five and had no choice.

So you wore it. And it got heavier. And heavier. And everyone around you appeared to be suffocating under their own backpack too, so you thought this was just life, this constant crushing weight, this never-ending act of enduring. Then one day someone says, "You know you can take that off, right?"

And you panic. Because without the backpack, you don't even know who you are and wonder if you even matter without it.

That's the Struggle Tax. It's the invisible weight we've been convinced we have to carry to prove we're worthy of taking up space.

And what's inside?

The stories of women who never rested and who were endlessly praised for it.

The belief that rest is lazy, selfish, and indulgent.

Every family saying that's outlived its purpose, like la lucha sigue and ser fuerte, that made us feel like we needed to be locked in 24/7.

The perfectionism that became your professional success strategy, because when you're the "only" in the room, every mistake feels as if it confirms what they already think about people like us.

The need to work twice as hard for half the recognition, while watching mediocre men get promoted around you.

The ever-persistent voice that echoes, every time you consider charging what you're worth or applying for that promotion, *Who do you think you are?*

The invisible scoreboard that says you haven't earned rest unless you've suffered enough first. It's like emotional credit scores; nobody knows how they're calculated, but somehow you're always behind on payments.

The impostor phenomenon that makes us feel like frauds every time we achieve something, as if someone were going to figure out you don't belong here.

The pressure to be "the good example," "the strong one," "the first one," or, my favorite, "the good one."

The weight of representing your entire community every time you walk into a boardroom or take the stage or go on national television for the first time.

Fear that if we set the obstacles down, we'll lose love, respect, and the station we've worked so hard to earn.

We carry these things like proof that we belong, proof that we've paid the cost of our dreams. But no one ever said we had to carry it, because the backpack was always optional.

Here's how to audit your own backpack: For one week, every time you feel resistance to something good (a compliment, an opportunity, rest), ask yourself, *"Could I be making this harder because I think I have to earn it?"* Write down what comes up. You'll begin to see a pattern.

The Possibility of Another Way

So, what do we do with this backpack? What do we do with the stories, the burden, the belief that our value is tied to our strife?

We start by questioning the weight. Not by dropping it all at once, but by noticing what's inside, and asking ourselves, *Who packed this?* (Chances are, you didn't even get to choose what went in there in the first place.)

Was it your mother's exhaustion? Your abuela's sacrifice? That friend who said you had to work twice as hard to get half as far? That voice in your head that says, "Not yet," "I'm not ready," "I'm not enough"? (That voice, by the way, is a terrible life coach.)

You're Paying the Struggle Tax When

You apologize for good news.

You work late to "prove" you deserve success.

You feel guilty when things come easily.

You add unnecessary steps to simple processes.

And then, little by little, we begin to loosen the straps.

This is not denial or spiritual bypassing. I will never say "just be positive" or "choose joy" without reckoning with what came before. I know what came before; I lived what came before.

My wounds, my grief, my challenges, they shaped me and they led me here. They gave me the tools I needed to build this life. But somewhere along the way, it registered that suffering is not the point of my life, and it's not the point of your life either.

Things began to change when I stopped seeing my pain and

everything I'd endured as the price of admission and started wondering what else might be possible.

I'm not saying suffering isn't real. I *am* saying it shouldn't be glorified.

You don't have to prove your worth through exhaustion, and you don't have to apologize for wanting more ease.

The most radical thing we could do, in cultures that revere endurance, is to choose softness. Not because life is soft (mine has been anything but soft), but because we are done letting our difficulty be our only currency. We don't have to keep paying the Struggle Tax to be deserving of happiness.

Ease is not the opposite of being strong. It's what allows us to stop bracing for the worst and finally start living.

EDA and the Faces of Struggle

In the Eñye Dream Accelerator (EDA), I watched the same story play out in different costumes. There was the endless credential-chasing, the exhaustion worn like a badge of honor, the perpetual waiting for "perfect timing." Different strategies, same invisible belief system: I haven't suffered enough to deserve this yet.

None of them understood they were doing this. The hardship conditioning was so embedded, so woven into their understanding of how the world worked, that questioning it never occurred to them. It wasn't conscious—it was just how things were. How they'd always been. I recognized it immediately because I'd lived my own version of this same pattern.

Each woman was brilliant, capable, and absolutely ready for more. But they'd all internalized their own particular way to delay their worthiness—their own dialect of "not enough yet." Like watching different actors delivering the same monologue. Each woman had her own way of delivering the lines, all working from the same script, a "truth" we absorbed without realizing it.

Nobody warns you that breaking generational patterns can make your community resent your freedom. When you stop struggling, you become a mirror for everyone still trapped in the cycle. Your ease becomes their discomfort. Your success, evidence of their perceived limitations. So like crabs in the bucket, they try to pull you down, not from malice, but because your liberation feels to them like abandonment.

I wish I could tell you there's a perfect script for handling this, but no explanation will satisfy someone who needs you to stay small so they can feel safe. The real work is trusting yourself to keep growing when they say, "You've changed."

The Rip Current of Worthiness

For seventeen years, I told myself I wasn't ready to make my documentary. Not fluent enough in Spanish. No film degree. Not qualified in experience or academically. I believed I would not be taken seriously.

But beneath all those surface-level reasons was something harder to distinguish and nearly impossible to see. It wasn't just that I lacked the right credentials, it was that I didn't believe I'd suffered enough to deserve telling the story.

Some part of me believed there had to be someone else, someone with a harder life, a deeper sacrifice, a more "authentic" journey, who was more qualified to make the film. Until I could match that level of suffering, I hadn't earned my place at the table.

That's how this belief system works. It's like a rip current, invisible to the eye, but violently disorienting once you're caught in it. You think you're swimming toward shore, toward success, toward self-expression, toward fulfilling a lifelong dream, but the harder you kick, the farther you get pulled out into the ocean of earned worthiness and the more exhausted you become.

You start to believe maybe the problem is you. That you're not working hard enough, are not a strong enough swimmer, or maybe you should have gone out later in the day. You don't notice it's the current (that you couldn't see) that's dragging you out and the collective belief that difficulty is a precondition for visibility. Like blaming yourself for the weather.

And so you delay. You say, "Not yet." You imagine there's a version of you that will "one day" feel ready, until one day is seventeen years later and it hits you that what you've been waiting for is enough suffering to justify stepping forward and taking up space. Seventeen years of dress rehearsals for a show that was always ready to open.

But we don't escape a rip current by swimming harder. We get free first by noticing it. Then by shifting course and swimming parallel to shore, instead of straight toward it, until the pull weakens. Until you find your strength again.

This chapter is your moment to notice. To stop confusing setbacks with readiness. To stop paying for your worth in pain.

Because your voice was never supposed to be earned. It was always yours.

The Hidden Cost of Purpose-Driven Work

I have a love-hate relationship with Instagram, but if it weren't for that platform, I would never have met Rosalia. Usually it just shows me ads for things I mentioned three hours ago, but occasionally it delivers actual high-quality humans worth knowing.

Rosalia reached out asking for votes for a contest. I rarely respond to those kinds of appeals, but something made me stop scrolling long enough to hear her out and vote for her. I sent her a quick note afterward, not to pat myself on the back but because it took courage to make that video, and I wanted her to know I was rooting for her.

I had no idea what a big part of my life she would later become.

She joined EDA with a vital and urgent idea: a platform where survivors of sexual assault could learn how to teach their kids about consent. She'd started with a podcast but felt pulled to build something bigger. Coming off what she'd considered a "failed" business, she was still processing the disappointment.

I knew she was onto something massive and I wanted to do whatever I could to support her. During one coaching session, she said, "Give it to me straight, Denise. Don't candy-coat it. I need some tough love; I can take it."

"I don't do tough love anymore; I just do love." And I coached her through the situation. This came up repeatedly, her asking for my feedback to be hard and me refusing. I'd spent too many years believing that growth required harshness and I wasn't going to perpetuate that with her.

During one call where she was feeling particularly challenged, I told her, "One day your name will be synonymous with the word *consent*. People won't be able to talk about this topic without acknowledging your work. You'll see." And I believed it.

She went on to become hugely successful, eventually serving as a founding member and board chair for the largest survivor-centered global movement working to end child sexual abuse and exploitation in the world, the Brave Movement. Even then, she could hardly believe it was because she was the most qualified. She had over 188,000 Instagram followers and was collaborating with the biggest names in parenting. Yet when this group of global thought leaders believed she was the perfect choice to lead them, she felt underprepared for the job. Surely, she should be more accomplished to be worthy of that position. Because apparently having almost two hundred thousand followers and international recognition wasn't quite enough evidence.

The ghost of el qué dirán haunted her every move to build a sustainable business. Even as she helped thousands, she would receive DMs asking, "How dare she put a price tag on healing"—as if her bills didn't exist, as if sustainability wasn't necessary for longevity.

Each criticism hit a nerve, triggering that deep-rooted belief that purpose-driven work should come at a personal cost. That if you're really committed to the community, you should give until it hurts. The more impact she made, the more entitled people felt to her labor, her knowledge, and her carefully crafted resources.

But here's where Rosalia chose triumph. She stopped letting other people's discomfort with her success dictate her prices. She chose to value her work based on its impact, not on how much she had sacrificed to offer it.

This was the pattern at its most insidious, the belief that work born from trauma, from community need, from genuine purpose, must be given away rather than sustainable service. That choosing to thrive while doing healing work was somehow a betrayal of its origins. As if being broke somehow made you more noble.

Rosalia's journey mirrors what I discovered in that Safeway parking lot, that the very belief system designed to keep us humble was actually keeping us small. The choice to triumph meant questioning everything we'd been taught about earning our worth and daring to believe we could change the world and support ourselves.

Here's what Rosalia learned about pricing without the Struggle Tax. Your personal pain doesn't make your work less valuable—it makes it *more* valuable. Price things based on the transformation you create, not the guilt you feel about its coming as a result of your trauma.

Collective Permission

What I've learned from watching these women transform is that breaking free from the Struggle Tax isn't just about individual liberation, it's also about making space for others to do the same.

Every time one of us chooses ease over suffering, claims success without apology, or dares to thrive without proving worthiness through pain first, we create a chain reaction. We become living examples. Like a reverse domino reaction, each one standing up, instead of falling down.

I see it happening in real time. When Rosalia claims her seat at the table without apology, other Latinas start seeing their own power differently. When these women choose to thrive openly, something shifts in our community.

Success is not a limited resource.

What We're Building

The women in my programs aren't just launching businesses or creating platforms, they're building something totally different from what we were taught. Where worthiness is something you don't have to earn. Where success doesn't require suffering, ease stops feeling suspicious, and belonging comes from authenticity, not shared pain. They're rewriting the rules we never agreed to follow in the first place.

And maybe that's the legacy our ancestors were really fighting for all along. Not so we could keep struggling, but so we could finally effing stop.

Choosing Our Battleground

This isn't about ignoring systemic racism or pretending structural barriers don't exist. It's about recognizing where we have power to change things *now*. Because waiting for the world to change while we stay stuck accomplishes nothing. Some battles we can win immediately, others will take lifetimes.

Let's start with the ones we can actually control.

This is why I'm so passionate about challenging gatekeeping around Latinidad through language, and why I'm showing you exactly how this struggle narrative has a much bigger hold on our lives than we realize. The external barriers are real, but we can start breaking down the internal ones right now. Two fights happening simultaneously, but only one we can win today.

The choice is yours. Keep proving your worth the hard way or finally accept you're worthy of what you desire.

When you choose triumph over struggle, you change your life and what's possible for everyone watching.

The Collective Recognition: Ripples of Permission

What moves me most deeply in this work isn't just the individual breakthroughs, it's watching everyone having this "holy shit" moment together. It's what happens when women dare to believe that maybe we don't have to fight so hard to deserve what we desire and you can see the permission wash over everyone else's face. Like watching a roomful of people remember they're allowed to take up space.

It's my oxygen.

I saw it in every cohort of EDA. The moment when someone shared their passion without first listing their hardships. The collective exhale when a member shared a success without apologizing for it. The tears that flowed when someone finally admitted they were tired of making everything so hard and just priced their program at what they knew they deserved.

The space we created together allowed them to find words for what they'd always felt and the freedom to want more. Courage is contagious.

The Power of Fierce Love

But here's what breaks these patterns most powerfully: love.

I experienced this fierce love in action after a particularly memorable keynote in Chicago. I stayed one extra night and attended a party on the last night of the conference. As I was leaving the room where just twenty-four hours before I'd delivered a keynote about belonging to four thousand attendees, a small group gathered around me.

Connecting with attendees post-keynote about their identity, holding space as I listen to their dreams and of course their secrets, is one of my favorite parts of being a speaker. One of the gentlemen leaned over and said, "I have a question for you that I hope is okay to ask."

"Sure, ask away." Bracing for impact, hoping for something real.

"When you were up there talking about belonging, I was wondering, 'Would you say you were talking about love?'"

He saw straight through to the heart of my work, and I'm not sure I've ever received a higher compliment. My ribs expanded, making room for a breath I didn't know I was holding. I let it out slowly.

"Yes. Exactly, yes. I *was* talking about love."

I wasn't a keynote speaker before all of this. Just someone deeply passionate about making sure people felt seen. That's what I set out to do and that's what I keep doing. You'd be surprised what happens when people who once felt invisible suddenly feel recognized. It's miraculous and addicting to play any role in that kind of knowing.

That's what I'm talking about when I say love transforms these patterns. Fierce love that sees you fully—all your inherited bullshit *and* your power. Your ancestors' struggles *and* your right to have some damn ease in your life.

This love refuses to let you pile on extra drama when you're already fighting systems designed to keep you small. It holds your truth without sugarcoating anything or making it smaller to make others more comfortable.

Look, being hard on ourselves has never been good for us.

This is what choosing triumph over struggle actually looks like day-to-day. It's not a big overhaul but instead a simple decision to stop being your worst enemy.

Our Collective Liberation

This internal work isn't just about individual success; it's how we all get free, together. When we do the hard work of dismantling our own struggle patterns, we don't just free ourselves. We free our communities. We participate in the ancient work of repairing what's been torn apart, one soul at a time, one family line at a time, one generation at a time.

Every woman who stops proving herself through suffering, who chooses ease without apology, who dares to thrive openly, becomes a living testament that there's another way, and you're allowed to choose it too. This is how real change happens—not through preaching, but living it.

And it works from the inside out, not the outside in. We can't dismantle systems of oppression while still keeping ourselves small with the same beliefs those systems taught us. When we stop oppressing ourselves, we show up differently for the collective fight. Remember what Debbie Ford showed me: The universe is holographic—heal one part, and you heal the whole.

Freedom isn't selfish when it creates more freedom for everyone else.

She chooses not to struggle, and instead, she triumphs.

Reflection: What Are You Ready to Put Down?

You've carried it long enough. That voice that says you haven't suffered enough to deserve what you want. The belief that struggle is the price of admission to your own life. The invisible backpack packed with everyone else's expectations of how hard things should be for you.

Here's what I want you to try:

Instead of asking "Am I ready?" or "Have I earned this?"—ask yourself, "What would I choose if I believed I was worthy right now?" Not someday, not after you've proven yourself *yet again,* but right now.

Write down whatever comes up, for example, the business idea or creative project you've been sitting on for years, the boundary you're afraid to set, the price you're afraid to charge (or the salary you're afraid to ask for), the dream you've convinced yourself you are not "qualified" for yet.

Think about what stops you. Those familiar refrains, "Not yet" or "I'm not ready" or "Who do you think you are?" Those are the things we're going to put down.

Here's the part that might surprise you: Instead of trying to hate those limiting beliefs, I want you to appreciate them. Not because they were good for you, but because they kept you safe when you needed safety. They pushed you forward when you needed pushing. And now with a clear mind, you get to choose which ones stay and which ones go.

You've already proven you can handle everything that life has thrown your way. The question isn't whether you deserve ease and joy, you absolutely do. The question is, Are you ready to stop making yourself prove it over and over?

What would it feel like to move through just one day without that crushing weight on your back? Start there.

Listen to me, you were *always* bigger than whatever you've been carrying. Time to remember that.

CHAPTER TEN

Never Choose Yourself over What's Expected:
Living as a Liberated Woman

If you've ever felt guilty for wanting more than you were given, you'll understand what I'm about to tell you.

I used to think liberation meant leaving. But liberation isn't about walking away from your life; it's about walking toward the woman you've always been but were afraid to become.

For decades, I confused freedom with distance. I thought the solution to feeling trapped was geography—new cities, different relationships, better circumstances. But the woman I was running toward was never in another place; she was buried inside the life I was already living, waiting for me to stop making excuses and let her the eff out.

She wasn't always polite. She wasn't compliant. She had opinions that made family dinners unbearable and dreams that demanded I disappear from everyone else's needs for months at a time.

She was the storyteller who needed to document the truth, even when it shook the room. The speaker who said what no one else would say. The writer who refused to protect anyone's feelings at the expense of her own integrity.

But she didn't come without consequences.

She ruined some things. She cost me people and rattled my reputation. And I almost didn't let her out.

But the grief of not becoming her started to feel heavier than the fear itself.

This chapter isn't just about putting yourself first. It's about claiming what's wild, deep, and pressing inside you, that song that's been playing softly in the background your whole life. The one you've been keeping at whisper volume because everyone else prefers you be accommodating. Liberation is finally turning up your own music, even when people complain it's too loud.

And it starts when we choose the self that might cost us everything and decide to fight for her anyway.

The "Good" Latina's Playbook

She was born on a rainy night in North Miami.

I didn't know I was pregnant with her. But she'd been growing inside me for years, hidden under years of being told to be grateful for what I had, even if it was hardly anything.

She arrived without fanfare, at a wooden table that felt sturdy under my arms.

We were swapping funny stories, medicine for the soul, until Carlos reached into the air between us. "Have any of you ever felt like you were not . . . Latino enough, because your Spanglish is better than your Spanish, or because you don't know how to cook, or dance, or know all the things?"

The volume in the entire bar dropped and everything snapped into focus. It felt undeniable, immediate, and visceral. My entire body vibrated with excitement; every cell knew this was my next step. I felt grounded, certain, and alive.

People need to know this feeling and I'm going to be the one who tells them. I need to make a movie about this.

I didn't know how or who would help. But it didn't matter. The clarity was louder than the fear, just for a second.

The drive home was only forty minutes, but by the time I reached Coconut Grove, the familiar voice was back. . . .

Who do you think you are? You're broke. Driving a beat-up pickup with no air-conditioning. You work above a printing press that smells like ink and dust and old ways of doing things. Filmmakers don't come from places like this. They don't look like you. Their lives don't look like this.

For seventeen years, she pounded on that door. Every time I got close to opening it, the fear would pull me back. Until one day the pounding got louder than the fear.

I thought I could bury her for good.

But the wild woman within us never really disappears.

The dutiful good girl had a whole system for keeping her in line. Get the stable job, with benefits. Pick a good guy who looked great on paper, even if something always felt off. Stay grateful. Don't ask for too much. Don't dream too big.

I'd always played with the edges of my identity, pushing boundaries, questioning things, but these invisible beliefs were harder to shake. They lived in a place I couldn't reach; I could only see and feel the result of my adherence to them.

The dutiful Latina convinced me that wanting more was selfish. That dreaming of big stages, and cameras, and telling stories that mattered, was self-centered and indulgent when I should be focused on stability, security, the things that accommodating young women prioritize.

She said, *You're already doing better than your parents ever imagined. Isn't that enough? Why do you need more?*

And that voice wrapped itself around my ambition like a noose.

Every time the wild filmmaker stirred, at film festivals where I felt my chest tighten with longing, during award shows where I watched people accept recognition for taking the exact risks I was too afraid to take, the compliant version of me would yank it tighter.

That's not for people like us. That's not how our story goes.

She was getting harder to contain.

If I wanted to become the woman who woke up that night in the bar in North Miami, I would have to betray the good daughter, before she buried us both.

What Liberation Looks Like

It was Irisneri, a genealogist, who first showed me not just how deeply this pattern runs, but how powerfully it could be transformed.

In our EDA coaching container, her story became our mirror, reflecting back both the cost of what we'd been given and the possibility of choosing differently. She showed us that choosing your wild calling isn't an act of rebellion; it's an act of generational legacy repair.

Irisneri didn't just research family trees. She healed generational fractures by helping people reclaim lost pieces of themselves and reconnecting them to roots that had been severed by immigration, war, and shame. Her work provided a bridge between past and present, helping families understand how their stories shaped their identities.

The irony wasn't lost on me: Here was a woman whose gift was freeing others from limiting family patterns while she remained trapped in one herself.

She was brilliant at her work, exceptionally capable, already changing lives. But she couldn't officially start her business, not really, because she wasn't certified yet.

"What would be different after the certification?" I asked her.

Her answer was heartbreakingly simple: She'd finally feel fully credentialed to charge people. That's it. It had nothing to do with skill or experience. Genealogy was her magnificent obsession; she'd do it for free and did.

But something deeper was happening. As Latinos in the United States, we're already under scrutiny—around our legal status, around accents, around people being impatient when our parents don't speak English well or at all. So our parents teach us: Don't make waves, don't attract attention to yourself.

Well-behaved daughters become the family's shield. We follow every rule, check every box twice, earn our place through channels no one can question. We become the model citizens that prove our family's worthiness, the interpreters who navigate hostile systems without causing friction, the steady achievers who minimize the family's visibility to potentially dangerous attention.

You don't claim your power—that draws the wrong kind of scrutiny. You wait to be given permission, preferably with official documentation that no one can challenge.

Irisneri had internalized this strategy so completely that even in her calling to heal generational trauma, she was trapped by it. The endless certifications weren't about competence—they were armor against a system that already questioned her right to be here, to speak with authority, to claim expertise.

She was collecting hall passes for her own dreams. Institutional approval that would protect her from the question that haunts so many of us: "Who do you think you are?" But when she finally laughed, the armor didn't just crack, it fell off completely. Her shoulders visibly dropped and her real presence filled the space between us.

That question she'd been armor-plating against isn't just personal for women like us—in our case, it carries the weight of our families and our community. Are we bringing unwanted attention? Being too loud, too visible, too much for people already under siege?

The Moment She Chose Her Wild

Breaking generational programming is no small feat. It's all but impossible to do alone. Even in community, there has to be genuine trust, and I had that with Irisneri. But that didn't mean I could get her there. She had to meet me halfway, and she did.

The opening came during one of our group calls. She was preparing to apply for the certification program, still months away from feeling "ready."

"You're going to get it, right? The certification?" I asked.

She nodded. Of course. She always did what she said she would.

"Okay, so let's fast-forward. Tomorrow, someone reaches out desperate for what you offer, a family searching for their roots, needing healing you can provide. Would you say no?"

She paused. We could feel the virtual space tighten. All the unspoken rules rising and filling the tension. Everyone in EDA recognized it. The part where you feel the calling . . . and the fear of what it might cost you.

And then she laughed. Her joy cracking something open for all of us. The invisible weight she'd been shouldering wasn't hers anymore. She started laughing and said, "Oh my God, I've been standing in my own way this whole time."

Because the truth had been there all along. She wasn't waiting on the certification. She was waiting to feel safe enough to step outside the mindset that had protected her family for generations. She was waiting to feel safe enough to be visible, to claim authority, to risk the scrutiny that comes with success.

In that moment, she made a choice that would have terrified every good daughter who came before her: She decided to trust her own knowing over the external validation that had always been the daughters' shield. She chose to claim her power without the armor of official approval.

Not because she felt ready, but because she recognized that feeling would never come—not when readiness meant risking everything her family had unknowingly taught her to avoid.

The Cost of Choosing Wild

¿Quién se cree que es?—that question carries different weight when your family is already under scrutiny. When being too exposed, too successful, too bold, could bring unwanted attention.

By choosing to start before she was "officially ready," Irisneri was allowing herself to move beyond that belief. In immigrant families, you can struggle together, but individual success can feel like abandonment of the collective shield. Better to stay "almost ready" than risk exposing the family to judgment.

But Irisneri chose her wild calling anyway. Started charging for her gifts. Made enough to quit her job. Built a waiting list of people desperate for the healing and answers that only her expert research could provide.

The woman who helped others reclaim their roots finally claimed her own, not by abandoning the ones she came from, but the ones she's planting now.

Her courage forced me to reckon with a brutal truth: Even after all my progress, I was still afraid.

Asking Uncomfortable Questions to Get What You Deserve

A few years later, I was on a Zoom call with a women's ERG leadership team. All white women, except for one very junior level Latina, who was championing me as their keynote for an upcoming event. You know the drill, they wanted me to "inspire diverse talent" but they didn't have much budget.

As they explained the women's leadership initiative, they mentioned how supportive their male executive sponsor was. *Wait, their male sponsor?* So I asked, "Are there women at his level who could champion this?" They actually laughed, as if having a male sponsor for a women's advancement event wasn't strange at all.

Out of curiosity, I pressed further: "What does the board look like? How many women are on it, and how diverse is it?"

"Well, out of twelve board members, there is one white woman and one man of color." That was it. Ten white men making decisions about inclusive initiatives they wanted me to support while cutting my fee.

I hadn't shared my rate yet, and truth be told, if they'd approached this differently, with real respect for the work, I might have been more flexible. But something about asking me to discount my expertise while having ten white men oversee their diversity efforts felt off.

So I said, "I'm probably out of your budget," and shared my full rate. And just like that, the conversation ended, and I didn't feel bad about it. Because this is what living from your worth looks like in professional spaces—refusing to subsidize the appearance of change.

This means remaining steadfast to that part of you that recognizes when something's not right. You hold your ground on your worth when people try to talk you down, knowing when to walk away because you trust you were made for something better.

Success on Our Own Terms

Maybe you're wrestling with this same question I was: How do you stay authentically Latina while succeeding in spaces that weren't built for us? How do you honor your culture without being labeled "too much"? I've learned that authenticity is about knowing your worth so deeply that you don't need external validation to prove it.

When I shared my full fee, I wasn't abandoning my Latino values of humility. I was honoring the Latino value of taking care of my family by ensuring I got paid what I was worth.

The strategy isn't to abandon your cultural values and become fully "Americanized." It's to redefine what knowing your worth looks like in your career. That sometimes means asking uncomfortable questions and walking away from opportunities that don't value you and standing firm in your worth, *in every conversation.*

Reflection: What We're Worth

The patterns we've explored in our families don't stay in our families. They follow us into boardrooms, salary negotiations, and every professional moment where we're asked to put a price on our contributions. Here's how to break the pattern where it hits your bank account hardest, in your next money conversation.

Ask for the full amount. Not 10 percent less, not the "reasonable" discount you think makes you more likable. The full amount. Remember that what protected our abuelas in their world can limit us in ours.

Practice saying, "I'd like to discuss compensation," without apologizing first. Present your case without hedging with phrases like "I know this might be a stretch, but . . ." Instead, take a beat and sit in the uncomfortable moment after you make your ask—whatever you do, do not immediately offer to accept less.

The goal isn't to be more aggressive, it's to *stop confusing self-advocacy with aggression.* A direct request to be paid what you are worth is not an attack and doesn't mean you are taking something from someone else. It's a business conversation about fair compensation based on the value you bring. Period.

This confusion happens for real reasons. We were taught values such as respeto, humildad, and familismo—and speaking directly can feel as if we're crossing the line. Adding to that, assertiveness in women of color is often mislabeled as aggression, so we're already fighting against perceptions that don't match our intentions. Self-sacrifice was and continues to be praised. That safety reflex is rooted in our nervous system. It makes sense that it will take effort to do something different. But it's worth trying.

You are worth the discomfort of your own growth.

Start small if you need to. Let's begin with requesting a title that matches your responsibilities or negotiating a flexible schedule that lets you be present for your family. You don't have to leave your Latinidad at the door to be successful! It's time to stop making our professional worth conditional on how little we're willing to accept.

For entrepreneurs, this programming shows up in our pricing, but the reasons run deeper than just wanting to be nice. We were taught that asking for more than you need is greedy and that "good people" don't put money before relationships. We get preoccupied with not overcharging instead of what our results are worth.

Add to that the reality that when women of color charge premium prices, we're more likely to be seen as "money hungry" or as "taking advantage." We preemptively discount ourselves to avoid that judgment. And while we're here, let's acknowledge we watched our moms, our tías and abuelas, work for far less than what they were worth, grateful for whatever they could get. And don't come at me for saying this, but that "gracias a Dios que tengo trabajo" mentality keeps us broke.

Your client who lands the big promotion after working with you, the entrepreneur who finally launches after months of your coaching, the opportunity of a lifetime that you helped your client negotiate—you provided that space and it changed the trajectory of their lives. But here we are pricing our life-changing work at $500 when it's worth $5,000 or $50,000 because we're more afraid of being called expensive than we are of staying small.

Mujer, the work that you do changes lives. Stop getting paid as if you're just doing favors.

DENISE SOLER COX

Choosing Your Story

The conversation happened before we even went into production, when *being eñye* was still just an idea that I desperately longed to make real. I was so ready to give a voice to something I'd been carrying for years. The story of first-generation identity, the unique struggles of being caught between worlds, the weight of preserving culture while making good on your parents' sacrifice.

But I didn't know anything about making a movie, and I didn't have a single connection in the industry. Once the idea came to me in the bar in North Miami in the late nineties, it took seventeen years before I had the guts to do anything about it. Then, one day, in 2012 at a playdate when my girls were in preschool, a woman mentioned that her neighbor was an Academy Award nominee. It would take me five months to work up the courage, but I finally asked for his information and pitched him my film idea.

Though busy in preproduction with his own film, he made time to listen and meet with me once or twice afterward. When he needed help with the theatrical release of his latest project—a documentary about wild horses—he hired me to help with marketing. Here I was, a Puerto Rican girl from New York, working on a film about wild horses, which my husband, from Oklahoma, could relate to (his father used to buy and break wild horses), but which had nothing to do with anything I knew. But it didn't matter. I had my way in.

I decided to be a sponge and learn everything I could. I lost track of the hours and worked every weekend. After several years of being home with my girls, I was learning how to balance full-time work that I loved with being a mom, even when dinner wasn't cooked because I was still at the office.

I slid into meetings and contributed value whenever I could, adopting a beginner's mentality where I had no problem not knowing the vernacular or understanding all the professional acronyms. My strategy was simple: I'd do whatever needed to be done, hoping they'd let me stay and soak it all in.

By the time that chapter ended, I understood the basic ins and outs of documentary distribution, though I'd have so much more to learn about the production side when I coproduced and codirected my own film.

I approached *being eñye* the same way I've tackled everything else that mattered, with relentless determination and every culturally coded superpower our community is known for. I had a real opportunity and I wasn't going to let it pass me by. For eighteen months I worked nonstop, fueled by our Latino work ethic, creativity, love for community, and resourcefulness, and an obsessive passion for the story we were telling.

I left nothing on the table. I turned over every metaphorical stone, squeezed every last drop from opportunities that came our way—I gave it everything I had. It was exhausting, yes, but also life-giving. I've never experienced anything like it before or since.

I vetted every subject and interviewed each one. I built relationships from scratch—one connection with access to a professional studio in Manhattan offered us forty-eight hours to shoot back-to-back interviews, saving us thousands in production costs. I didn't know these people before the project. I just kept showing up. Every night I sent emails and knocked out to-do lists. Every morning I woke up and did it all again. I sat with editors, helped flag the gold from the interviews, chased down song rights we couldn't afford, and tracked down the artists who recorded the songs.

I finally crashed from exhaustion on a couch in a Bushwick studio while musicians laid down original music with my creative partner.

But even then I couldn't stop. I secured locations, such as the Cuban restaurant in Denver we used for a reenactment scene, and ran the casting call that included recruiting my hairdresser and her best friend because we needed more people. I worked closely with Charles (from chapter seven) on the film poster, and for the next several years I showed up at every screening.

Grit doesn't even begin to cover it.

Owning your story is just the beginning. You also need the strength to defend it, no matter what. Every rejection is an opportunity to learn resilience. All feedback is an invitation to grow. But most important, trusting where the message is coming from, deep down in your soul, and protecting that truth even when others try to diminish your vision will be crucial.

I thought everyone would understand. I thought the community would rally behind a story that had been living in the shadows for so long.

I was wrong.

The person who delivered the ultimatum was influential in Denver's Latino community. Someone whose support could open doors or close them. She didn't mince words: Unless we focused on the immigrant experience, the crossing, the life-and-death journey of getting here, we would lose all of her potential support, and in Denver's Latino community, her endorsement was worth more than money.

"*That's* the story that needs to be told," she said. "*That's* what people need to understand."

I felt my stomach drop. Not because she was wrong about the importance of immigrant stories, because those stories are vital and necessary. But because of what she was really saying, that the story of their children, our story, wasn't worthy of its own film.

The immigrant experience had become the only Latino narrative that felt legitimate to tell. Everything else was somehow lesser, not dramatic enough, not urgent enough. As if our identity struggles, our cultural navigation, our unique burden of being responsible for both preserving culture and justifying our parents' sacrifices, as if all of that was just a footnote to the "real" story.

I sat with her ultimatum for days. I could feel the familiar pressure to accommodate, to edit my vision to make others comfortable. The good Latina daughter in me urged, "Just do what she wants. Make it easier. Why make this harder than it has to be?"

But something wilder was awakening. The same voice that had woken up in that North Miami bar years earlier, the one that said, *People need to know this feeling and I'm going to be the one who tells them.*

I called her back.

"The immigration story matters, I know that," I said. "But this film is about their children. The ones stuck in the middle, trying to be enough for our parents while figuring out who we actually are. That's the story we're telling and we're not going to change it."

The lack of response on the other end told me everything. She wouldn't be endorsing us.

It was devastating and clarifying all at once. Devastating because it confirmed what I'd always suspected, that this story somehow felt less worthy of attention. But clarifying because it forced me to confront a truth I'd been avoiding: If I wasn't willing to fight for this story, who would?

In 2016, the first-generation experience wasn't getting the attention it gets now. There weren't podcasts, YouTube channels, social media platforms dedicated to understanding what it means to be the bridge between your parents' world and the dream you're chasing. We were invisible, caught between the dramatic narrative of arrival and the so-called success stories of full assimilation.

So, I chose my story over their support. I chose the vision that had been burning in me for years over the one that would have been easier to fund, easier to promote, and easier to defend.

Years later, when I started talking about writing this book, the same pattern emerged. "You should include men," people said. "You should open it up beyond just Latinas. Think about how much bigger your audience could be."

But this book exists because thousands of Latina women have shared their stories with me. Their struggles with family dynamics that don't translate across cultures, their experiences of carrying generational patterns they couldn't articulate.

This isn't a book that happens to be about Latinas. This *is* the Latina story, told by someone who's been trusted with it over and over. To dilute it, to make it more "universal," would be to betray every woman who has shared her truth with me in conference hallways, who cried during coaching calls, who finally felt seen when I gave language to something she'd been carrying alone.

I refused to water it down. These women had trusted me with their truth, and I wasn't going to sell that out for a bigger audience.

Sometimes protecting your vision means losing support. Sometimes it means walking away from opportunities that would require you to compromise your truth. But editing your story to fit someone else's idea of what's important is a betrayal of everyone who trusted you with theirs.

The wild woman in me understood something crucial: Our stories already matter. They just need someone who won't back down from telling them.

The Certainty That Can't Be Shaken

When people ask me about my "accomplishments," they usually mean the external markers—the awards, the stages, the book deal, the recognition. And don't get me wrong, I love the accolades. I love the opportunities. It feels damn good when we're acknowledged for the work we do.

But we need to ground ourselves in something else.

The divine calling that shows us what's important every day.

What I own is something deeper, something that can't be given or taken away. The certainty that comes from being entrusted with people's most guarded truths, repeatedly, over many years. The people who have shared their secrets and dreams with me everywhere I go have validated my work more than anything else I've ever done.

This book exists because of what was revealed in those conversations. The patterns that emerged when women finally felt safe enough to share what they'd been living with alone showed me that the things we think make us feel broken are actually the things that make us human.

That repetition created an unshakable knowing in me, not arrogance, but earned expertise. When you've held people's shame told a dozen different ways over many years, you develop a conviction that can't be shaken.

And that confidence is what makes choosing your vision and choosing yourself possible. Because when you know, like really know, the value of what you carry, anyone else's approval becomes secondary to your own inner knowing.

The Moving Goalpost

Not until I was in my fifties, going through the most painful version of a midlife crisis, did I grasp I'd spent the majority of my life chasing something I could never catch.

The moving goalpost of "enoughness" had confined me for decades. First, enough meant moving out, leaving the dysfunction behind. Then it meant getting a job and being successful in Miami. Then it meant picking up and starting a whole new life in Denver. Then getting married, having a family, and making the documentary. Then winning awards. Then the speaking career. Then writing this book.

The trap was that I was chasing a version of "enough" that would never satisfy the people whose approval I was seeking. My family's version meant staying close, being available, putting family first no matter the cost.

And even deeper than that standard, I was unconsciously keeping satisfaction just out of reach because achieving it would mean confronting a terrifying truth—that leaving had been the right choice all along.

The magical moment of actually feeling adequate never came because I couldn't let it come. It was always moving, always just beyond my reach, keeping me safely trapped in the guilt I knew how to hold.

I was a chronically unsatisfied child who fantasized about being anywhere but where I was—older, different city, different life. Those daydreams got me through some dark times, but they also taught me that satisfaction was something you earned later, not something you felt now. Rest was selfish, and contentment was complacency.

I was keeping fulfillment at bay on purpose. Feeling satisfied would mean accepting that I'd made the right choice in leaving, and that would shatter the familiar guilt I'd been carrying like a security blanket. This guilt somehow felt safer than fully owning my choices.

The exhaustion of chasing worthiness versus the ease of simply *being* worthy is the difference between running uphill forever and finally reaching level ground. But I couldn't get there because that meant confronting a terrifying possibility: I was the one who got away.

This is the deepest taboo of all, believing you deserve to save yourself. I had lived in an environment where my unacceptable parts, my ambition, my voice, my needs, were never invited to the party. I smothered them to withstand the climate. But you cannot save something by burying it alive. If you keep your spirit underground for too long, it doesn't stay safe, it begins to decay.

I was finally digging myself out of the grave I had dug to keep the peace. Staying would have meant suffocating slowly and I wasn't willing to let my soul wither for the sake of being a "good" daughter.

In cultures where family identity trumps individual identity, *self-preservation* feels wrong. We're taught that good daughters sacrifice themselves on the altar of family loyalty.

It finally hit me that the guilt I'd been carrying was proof of what I'd been taught. True belonging will never ask you to shrink. And after decades of unconsciously abandoning myself to avoid the truth that leaving was the right thing to do, I was exhausted.

The real question wasn't "Am I enough?"—it was accepting that I already was. Which meant I'd been punishing myself for making the right choice all along.

Gravity and Liberation

For decades I was just going around in circles.

To face the success and legacy I wanted to pass down to my daughters would require me to fully believe in myself. And that meant accepting that I wasn't betraying anyone by finally doing exactly what I needed to do, listening to where my heart was telling me to go.

This insight is seismic when you've been addicted to never feeling enough. When "not enough" has been your drug of choice for decades because it's easier to doubt yourself than to own your power.

The Betrayal Trap

We stay trapped not because we can't see the way out, but because the way out requires us to face truths we aren't ready to handle. That we were wise enough to know we deserved better. That the relationship we were trying so hard to preserve was actually deeply unhealthy. We protect ourselves from these realizations until we're strong enough to face them. Some truths have to wait until we're ready, and thank goodness they do.

For me, living as a liberated woman day-to-day means I constantly catch myself in the old patterns such as overdoing, overgiving, questioning myself too much. These are old habits born from never feeling on stable ground, from feeling responsible for things that were never my responsibility to begin with. But now I see it happening, and I choose differently.

The deeper trap is when we ask, "What's wrong with me?"—because it's easier than asking if I've been protecting myself from truths I'm not ready to face. Which means accepting that I was wiser than I gave myself credit for. And maybe the relationship we were trying so hard to honor was the thing we needed to escape.

There's nothing wrong with us. We're allowed to say *basta*—"enough." We're allowed to have limits. Things we're willing to tolerate and things we're not available to put up with any longer. We can make our own rules. But if you are going to do that, you need to understand, it will be painful.

This is what keeps so many of us trapped.

It's not that we're explicitly taught this way of thinking, but somewhere along the way, we learn that our liberation is a betrayal of our family. That honoring our personal needs means we are abandoning our culture. That success without suffering is suspicious and that setting boundaries with family equals disloyalty.

But the very thing our culture considers *betrayal*, the individualistic world calls *courage*. The vulnerability I was taught to bury, others welcomed as strength. And the truth I was told to keep secret became the opening others didn't know they needed.

This isn't about choosing between your culture and yourself. It's about refusing to accept a version of your culture that, however lovingly and unintentionally, teaches you the only way to be is to blend in. It's about refusing to shrink to make others comfortable, even when that refusal is misunderstood as abandonment.

When you free yourself, you don't just change *your* life; you rewrite what's allowed for everyone watching. Your liberation is not defiance but instead a beautiful example of what's possible.

When Latinas ask me, "What does your mother think?," they aren't judging me. They are asking if it's allowed. If women like them can actively choose themselves and survive it. If there really is a path to freedom that doesn't require losing everything they love.

And the answer is yes. But it requires something radical: believing that your truth matters as much as everyone else's comfort.

The Final Choice

A few weeks after my stepfather's funeral, my aunt Carol called. She wanted to fly me to New York as a birthday surprise for my mother. I was in the car with my family when she asked, and suddenly tears began to spill down my face that I couldn't control. My mother had rejected my film, my choices, and most things about me. She was vocal about the details I'd gotten wrong about her life, and she clearly disapproved that I was no longer willing to play my former role. I'd stopped going to New York for the holidays and I no longer visited her regularly. But she was still my mom.

I wasn't crying from anger. I was grieving decades of fighting for a relationship that kept rejecting me. I'd pushed back, set boundaries, spoken up countless times. But I'd never walked away. Even when it hurt, even when it was toxic, I kept showing up because walking away felt like the one thing I would never do.

I'd been living by rules that said you can fight with family, you can disagree with family, you can get mad at your family, but you can never, ever abandon them. Love meant staying, period, no matter the cost.

"I don't think she'd see it as a gift. I'm sorry, I can't make it."

That was the day I gave myself permission to matter.

Choosing myself felt like breaking every cultural rule I'd been immersed in. The taboo wasn't against speaking up, I'd done plenty of that. It was against giving up. Against saying, ironically, "Enough." Against putting my peace over theirs.

Liberation doesn't always feel like freedom at first. It feels like loss. Like mourning the version of you who shape-shifted for love.

But that was the breakthrough. Finally, *finally*, coming home to myself, but also doing it with a broken heart. Grieving the mother I'd always hoped she could be, and the daughter I'd tried so hard to become.

In that grief I found something: permission. Not from her, from myself. That choice was not an ending, it was my awakening. A voice that no longer hesitates and a life that belongs fully to me.

This is what I choose now:

Joy that doesn't apologize.

Wholeness that doesn't shrink.

Daughters who never question their right to choose themselves.

The woman who finally believes she is enough, right now, as she is.

This is liberation. Messy, heartbreaking, and finally mine.

She chooses her liberation over approval.

CHAPTER ELEVEN

Don't Abandon Your Responsibilities for Selfish Dreams:

Reviving Old Dreams and Making New Promises

I was dancing to promises I'd made at sixteen, in a loft that would force me to choose between my fear and my dreams.

It was New Year's Day in Denver. The sun was cutting through the tall windows of the Acme Lofts, flooding thirty-four hundred square feet of a former candy-factory space turned dream loft. At one time or another, we lived in one of three different sprawling lofts downtown, but this one was my favorite. It felt like a reward. Proof of years of hustle and believing in something I couldn't yet see.

Georgie, about five at the time, would ride her bike with training wheels through the open floor plan, her rubber tires gliding across the restored original wooden floors making a faint muted sticky sound.

The Acme Building was built in 1909, back when people drove

Model Ts and times felt simpler (though I'm not sure that they really were). Sometimes I'd walk barefoot across the floors and feel connected to the workers who once stood here and wonder what they dreamed about during their shifts. I thought about the promises they made to themselves while their hands stayed busy and was curious if they looked out these same windows and imagined a whole different life.

The factory had closed decades before someone with vision had transformed it into lofts, the same year I graduated from university, in 1992. But walking those floors, I felt connected to the idea of taking something abandoned and making it beautiful again.

The baby grand piano in our living room played itself. All it needed was an old-school floppy disk, and it would spring to life with everything from classical music to eighties pop songs, including my favorite, "Rosanna" by Toto. The sun flooding the loft with an expansive, illuminating wash. It felt like availability. For the first time nothing was hiding, because nothing needed to hide.

More than once, I danced around that loft with my daughters, singing the words at the top of my lungs, my voice and their giggles rising up the exposed brick to the timber ceilings, filling the whole space. Dancing with them loosened something that had been wound tight around my heart. I moved unashamed and wild, using my body to show them exactly what freedom and joy look like.

New Year's Brunch

Before the guests arrived for our annual New Year's brunch, I sat alone at the dining room table, the one spot where I could see everything—

the kitchen, the living room, the piano, and downtown Denver waking up with the sun. I opened my notebook, as I did every year, and began scribbling goals for the next twelve months. It was a ritual I cherished. But when I reached the part where I usually wrote *make movie*, I froze.

I'd written it so many times before (sixteen years, to be exact) that I began to wonder if I even meant it anymore.

This dream was no secret. I'd shared it on all sorts of occasions with all kinds of people since the idea came to me in that bar in Miami. I shared it as if I were certainly going to do it, and I lived for the conversations that happened afterward, when people shared their stories with me and suddenly we weren't strangers anymore.

Making this film felt like my destiny. But even though I knew it would one day happen, it also felt as if I'd need to be a whole other person, with completely different relationships and resources, to do it. At the very least, a degree in filmmaking to be able to pull it off.

Over the last sixteen years, I'd grown frustrated with people who shared endlessly about their dreams but never took a single action toward making them come true. That morning, it became clear I'd become one of them. The hypocrisy was mortifying.

Writing it down yet again felt like admitting I'd been lying to myself. It meant acknowledging that all the practical reasons I'd given for not pursuing it were just fears, and if I had money to bet, I'd probably bet against myself that it would ever happen.

I was so disappointed in myself for letting self-doubt drive the direction of my life for so long, for delaying what I knew I was meant to do, for abandoning something that felt like oxygen every time I talked about it. So, that morning, I made a pact with myself.

One year to make "significant progress" on this film. If I didn't, I would let it go. I wouldn't write it again next year, and I wouldn't bring it up in conversations anymore. I'd let it die. That was the vow.

Two and a half years later, my film *being eñye* premiered, a thirty-seven-minute documentary that would change not just my career but my entire life.

When I First Tasted Freedom

Mrs. Trovato was the skinniest teacher at Somers High School. She was in her mid-thirties with straight brown hair that fell past her shoulders, high cheekbones, creamy white skin, and almond-shaped eyes that always looked at me as if she wanted to hug me, but she never did. One afternoon in late 1987, after Spanish Club, she handed me a brochure for a summer program at the Malaca Instituto in Spain and encouraged me to go.

I remember looking at it and immediately knowing there was no way my overprotective Puerto Rican mother would ever let me fly to Europe alone to "learn Spanish." Especially not when I had family in Puerto Rico who spoke it fluently and were more than happy to practice with me.

But somehow, she agreed. Maybe it was my stepfather, George, who had lived in Italy and understood the benefits of such a program, who'd convinced her.

That's how I found myself, at sixteen, flying alone to Málaga to study Spanish at a school that still exists on the Costa del Sol.

That trip was everything. Not just because I was far from home, but because for the first time I was free. I'd worked three jobs that summer, babysitting, admin work, and scrubbing crusty food off white ceramic dishes at Somers Manor, a nursing home in my hometown, to earn the $1,000 in spending money to fund my time abroad.

Once I was there, I had no curfew, no rules, and no one micromanaging my choices. Just buses to catch, beach days to plan, and a brand-new city to explore, and, of course, hours of Spanish class every day.

It was the first time in my life I experienced myself as separate from my mother.

I skipped class when I felt like it. I smoked cigarettes on the balcony of my room, while I walked to class, and on the beach. I felt powerful because choosing my life every day felt so good.

And somewhere in all that freedom I was feeling, I made a promise.

I will keep this alive. I will keep traveling. I will see the world. I will create a life where I feel this free, always.

Of course, sixteen-year-old me had no idea what keeping that promise would actually require, but I wasn't thinking about the cost of that promise then.

At sixteen, I just knew I felt more like myself in Spain than I ever had at home, and I wanted to keep feeling that way forever. I belonged there in a way I never had back home. No one asked where I was from or mispronounced my name. My identity wasn't questioned. I experienced full acceptance.

It was, without question, the best thirty days of my life.

And then I went home.

DENISE SOLER COX

A Promise Broken

When I got home, everything was different. It wasn't the usual post-travel letdown. It was something deeper and heavier. As if I had left freedom behind only to feel as if the walls of my life had closed in even tighter while I was gone.

The constant reminders that my father was gone, that I needed to be strong, the pressures of senior year and thinking about college, it was all disorienting. I'd left behind ease and a different rhythm. Coming back to the States felt like stepping into skin that no longer fit. By that time my older brother, Gogi, was out of the house and had been married for a few years. David and my mother were fighting more than they were getting along, and from one day to the next, he was gone. He moved into a garage apartment with a friend in Yorktown Heights to figure out his next move. He'd chosen not to go to college right away.

Three months after I got back, he died in that car crash.

There's no way to describe what that kind of loss does to a person and to a family already frayed. Only two of us were left in the house then, me and my mother rattling around in all that empty space (she wouldn't marry her second husband, George, until I graduated high school, so we lived together alone for almost two years). The girl who had felt limitless on the beaches of Málaga was now living with a grief that she couldn't put into words in any language. There was no escape and no map.

And the promise I had made to myself in Spain didn't disappear right away. It just faded. Like a song playing in another room, still there, but too far away to make out the lyrics. It felt silly to me to chase something that now felt so far away.

So, I stopped talking about seeing the world, I stopped allowing myself to daydream about what could be. Life became about surviving what was. And when you're surviving, you don't stop to make plans or let yourself dream about them. You stop believing there'll be a future and you bury them accordingly.

For years, I told myself I'd go back. That I'd pick up where I left off. That someday I'd return to the girl who had found a place where she belonged. But I never did. Not because I didn't long to, but because the version of me who made that promise got lost, and between you and me, I didn't know how to get her back.

Our dreams don't die like people, though. They wait. Sometimes for years. Sometimes for decades. Mine waited in the background, resurfacing through old notebooks, coming up in late-night conversations with my husband, showing up as the sharp pang of regret when I saw someone doing something I once swore I would do.

The Return

For years, I lived with that feeling. Not just grief, but the particular sadness that comes when you give up on yourself. When you tuck what you want away next to the trauma and convince yourself that living "a good life" means expecting less because life stopped feeling safe.

But those dreams were still waiting.

And then, one New Year's morning in Denver, I felt her again, that girl from Málaga. Sitting at our massive dining table in the Acme Lofts, sun pouring through the windows, my daughter's faint bike tracks still visible across the wood floors. I had my spiral-bound notebook open to the first page, writing my goals, same as I had every January.

When I got to *make movie,* I froze.

I'd written that phrase sixteen times before. Sixteen times I'd said it and sixteen times I'd done nothing about it. But something shifted that morning. I didn't just want the dream back; I wanted *me* back.

The deal I made with myself wasn't just about a film. It was about honoring that sixteen-year-old girl who had tasted freedom and promised herself she'd never forget how it felt. It was about proving that some promises are worth keeping, even when they take decades to fulfill.

And for the first time in years, I believed it would be.

After I kept that promise to myself and the film was complete, it opened doors I never expected. I went on tour, speaking about belonging and identity. I became an expert on the very thing my documentary was about.

But the real transformation wasn't professional. It was personal. Making that film awakened something in me that had been dormant for decades. That sense of possibility. That belief that I was worth fighting for. That the girl who had felt so alive in Spain was still there, waiting.

Freedom, with Conditions

Eight years after *being eñye* premiered, I signed a book deal. The same creative force that had driven me to make the film was now pulling me toward writing. When I joined a writing academy, a ten-month commitment that felt both daunting and necessary, I didn't even feel that I deserved to call myself a writer. I felt instant guilt about the money I'd invested for the academy, feeling that it should have gone to family needs, such as shoes for my kids, music lessons, their college fund, anything but my creative indulgence.

My inner critic was loud, reminding me I didn't have the credentials, the experience, or the pedigree. But something in me said yes. I stumbled into a community that wasn't just feeding my creativity, it was reshaping my identity.

Then I saw it, a page on their website with the details about a writing retreat in Cortona. A hilltop town I'd only seen in films, where writers would gather to work on their craft surrounded by centuries-old homes overlooking miles and miles of the lush, patchy, rolling green hills of Tuscany. I went back to that retreat page on the website and read every detail, more times than I care to admit. I could so easily picture myself there walking those streets, waking up to the sound of church bells floating through ancient windows every morning.

But my life obligations said not now. So I filed it away, as I had with so many other dreams.

For weeks I found myself mourning a version of myself who would absolutely go on European writing retreats. The woman I'd promised myself at sixteen I'd become, someone who walked through ancient cities, spoke different languages, said yes to adventures. Someone whose life was defined by creativity and expansion and community.

I always felt that another version of me was out there, actually living, but that wasn't my reality and I'd accepted that. Until an email arrived on an ordinary Thursday afternoon in early May.

"A spot just opened up. If you'd like to join us in Cortona, it's yours."

I read it three times before it sank in. Then, I closed my eyes and took my first real breath in months. The writing retreat in Tuscany, the one I'd secretly been visiting online, reading every detail, imagining myself there, was suddenly within reach.

My heart was racing as if I'd been offered something precious, because maybe I had been.

When I told Kevin, his response was immediate: "When we get opportunities like this, we need to say yes. You need to go!" Even with money tight, even with every practical reason to say no, he saw what I was just beginning to see. I'd made a promise to myself at sixteen, and this was my chance to keep it.

Those weeks felt like my past and present were finally meeting. *I am finally her,* I kept thinking. The book deal was signed, and now I was off to Italy to write.

Becoming Her, Again

But nothing, not the photos I'd found on the internet, not my wildest imagination, had prepared me for the actual feeling of walking through the streets of Cortona.

Every morning, just as I'd imagined, I woke to church bells, at exactly 7:00 a.m., and also children's joy and laughter, drifting up through the French doors of my second-floor bedroom balcony. An elementary school was on the street just below.

The view from my terrace stretched for miles and miles, rolling green hills that looked just like a favorite paint-by-numbers craft my girls and I had worked on together years before.

I felt grounded in Cortona, clear. Young again. As if I'd tapped into something I'd been searching for my entire adult life without even realizing it.

Travel, for me, has always been a metaphor for freedom. It started in Spain. That was the first time I felt fully untethered from everything that had ever tried to define me—family, culture, trauma, and expectation.

The moment I landed in Italy, something inside me clicked into place. I was her, the girl from Málaga, all grown up, still so curious, still bold, but wiser, more grounded, and more certain. I'd finally found my way back to myself.

The cold spaces I'd created around my brother's death, around my buried creativity, around what I believed I could have . . . they finally started warming up again.

As I walked under clotheslines heavy with wet denim and crispy white bed linens, my feet found a rhythm they hadn't felt in thirty years. Even on the uneven cobblestones I felt completely steady.

It was a physical click like a bone setting back into its socket after being dislocated for decades. My body remembered this feeling from Málaga, the sensation of walking on ground that had outlived empires, knowing I was exactly where I needed to be.

I'd made this promise to myself, when I still believed anything was possible, and it kept me going through some of my hardest seasons. I'd be lying if I said I hadn't started to wonder if it was still possible for me. If maybe she was already gone.

She wasn't. I was in Tuscany, writing. I was her.

Finding Her Again

That retreat to Italy was a return to a version of myself I hadn't seen in decades. But it wasn't the end of the story. Because reinvention isn't a single moment; we get to return to ourselves again and again.

We don't become the woman we dreamed of just once. We become her over and over, every time we remember who we are. Every time we keep a promise to ourselves, however small. Every time we step forward, even when everything around us feels hard as hell.

I'm writing this now, not from a mountaintop of arrival, but from the middle of a life that's still changing. A life that, just like yours, keeps evolving. Some of those surprises take my breath away. Some are heartbreaking, and some strip away things and people I never thought I'd lose.

The commitments we make to ourselves matter; I know this for certain. And if we're brave enough to honor them, they lead us exactly where we need to go.

The girl who felt limitless on those Spanish beaches is still here. Still curious. Still ready for the next adventure. And I always will be.

I thought that was the final chapter. Girl makes promise, girl keeps promise, happily ever after, the end. But a few months after I returned from Italy, my daughter taught me something that reframed everything I thought I understood about buried dreams and what really happens to the parts of ourselves that we lock away.

The Real Reason Success Feels Impossible

My now eighteen-year-old daughter, Georgie, has this habit of perching at our tiny kitchen counter while I clean up, sharing whatever's on her mind (and I secretly love it). It was 5:00 p.m. in winter, pitch-black outside and in the dining room behind her. She sat at her favorite spot at the counter, munching on chips and cracking open a can of her favorite seltzer, a completely mundane after-school moment. Fresh from AP Physics, she wanted to explain something called thermal equilibrium.

"Ma, think of it like this. You're in a cabin in the woods in December. It's freezing outside, but you've got a fire going inside, so it's really warm. Then someone opens the door and the room gets cold. Your first instinct is to yell, 'Stop! Close the door! Stop letting the cold in!' But that's not what's actually happening."

She gestured with her hands. "The cold isn't coming in, the warmth is flowing out. Heat always moves toward cold until everything balances out."

I made her explain it again.

And again.

And again.

I couldn't stay standing. I walked into the living room, lay down on the couch, and closed my eyes just to process what she'd just revealed about my own life. Because she'd given me language for something I'd been living my entire life.

Each secret we keep freezes another part of who we really are. The sexual assault that we never shared. The family addiction we pretended didn't exist. Our mental health struggles that made others uncomfortable. The financial shame of growing up poor or the crisis that devastated us as adults. The harassment we endured at work because we "needed the job." The difficult relationship we have with our mother that we never admitted wasn't what it "should" be because good daughters don't complain about their mothers.

And it wasn't just the painful stuff. We also froze the dreams—the career that would take us away from family expectations, the move across the country that felt like abandonment, the art we wanted to make but decided it was "impractical."

All of these used to be warm with our authentic heat. The doors were open and life force could flow freely. But cultural conditioning and, let's face it, societal conditioning taught us that so many things are still taboo. We don't talk about money problems, mental illness, family secrets, or relationships that look good from the outside but feel cold on the inside.

So we shut those doors, and after years of keeping them locked, we have no idea where to find the key. We've been living with the frozen parts for so long, some places are like walk-in freezers in restaurant kitchens, the kind you need a heavy coat to enter.

As I wrote this last chapter, Dolores Huerta, cofounder of the United Farm Workers Association, revealed that César Chávez sexually violated her twice in the 1960s. She kept it a secret for six decades.

At ninety-six, she chose to make her truth public. The backlash was immediate. Dolores's name has been dragged through the mud, with many calling her complicit for staying silent. Yet, I know that countless women who have been carrying their own frozen truth for decades suddenly felt less alone.

I know I did.

I shared about truth telling in chapter two. Private truth telling heals you and public truth telling heals the culture.

At ninety-six, Dolores chose to heal the culture—proving that no door should stay frozen forever.

You've made it to the end, amiga. If you could take away one thing from everything we've shared together on these pages, let it be this:

The cold spaces will wait for you. They are not lost causes. They're patient and loyal and holding your truth in suspended animation. And when you finally feel ready to open that door to let the warmth back in, you won't find a graveyard of failed dreams. You'll find parts of yourself that have been waiting to breathe again, ready to forgive you instantly for the time you've spent away.

You deserve to get warm. Not someday, right now.

I hope to meet you on the line of secrets and dreams. You can tell me how warm you've made your beautiful life and how you've turned your pain into the masterpiece of your existence.

This is why the exercise from chapter one matters so much, because it's the first step toward opening those freezer doors.

And yes, it's just a start.

At work you might begin by simply acknowledging a single truth you've been avoiding. Make a list of the rooms you've abandoned. Then ask yourself, What's the worst that could happen if I cracked open the door just a little and let some warmth back into one of these spaces?

Writing this book was one big act of opening every closed door in my house. The cold rushed out, the warmth rushed in, and I'm finally living.

Sacred Thermal Equilibrium

Once I understood thermal equilibrium, I finally saw why success can sometimes feel so impossible for women like us.

Every time we hear, "Good daughters don't upset the family," we lock away our hearts the way we do with our valuables in the hotel safe along with our voice and our right to choose ourselves.

The cultural programming is specific and relentless:

If it came easy, you didn't earn it.

Your trauma should stay private (it makes the family look bad).

Speaking your truth means betraying everyone who is counting on you.

We become experts at thermal control. We learn to keep our heat trapped and our authentic selves locked away in impenetrable cold storage. We convince ourselves we're being good daughters, loyal family members, protectors of the movement.

But thermal equilibrium doesn't bend to our cultural programming.

Your authentic truth will always try to flow back to the places you've abandoned. Your creativity will always try to defrost the dreams you've frozen. Your *real voice* will always push against the limits you've been taught to maintain.

This is why we feel so stuck, so tired, so disconnected from our power. We're not just fighting external barriers to success; we're fighting against the natural flow of our own energy. The natural order is expansion, warmth, growth—it takes enormous effort to keep things frozen. We're spending massive amounts of force keeping our heat contained when it's trying to warm the very spaces that need healing the most. The exhaustion we feel isn't from our attempts to move forward; it's from the constant energy required to hold ourselves back.

I watched this with every woman who shared her story with me. The moment she let her heat flow toward her cold spaces—the moment she spoke her truth—I could see the balance restoring. The relief in her shoulders. The light returning to her eyes. The way she stood taller after being witnessed.

But I was still fighting the natural flow. Still keeping my heat trapped, still maintaining those frozen places where my secrets lived.

Story after story, I watched women reconnect with something deeper in our culture—resilience, unwavering loyalty, the power of testimonio. Yes, we were taught to keep family secrets, but we were also given compadrazgo. Our ancestors didn't survive by staying silent forever; they survived by knowing when and where it was safe to share their truths, by creating spaces where stories could be held safely, by understanding that healing happens in community.

Even with this deeper wisdom, I could see the cost of what we'd been taught reflected in their eyes. How we use buried pain as a reason to stay stuck. How we turn frozen dreams into evidence that we're not meant for more. How we mistake our programmed endurance for strength.

The sheer volume created pressure I couldn't ignore.

This book exists because truth won't stay buried forever. Just ask Dolores Huerta.

And watching women heal made me examine my own cold spaces. I began to see that I needed to share my stories too—not just to warm my own frozen places, but so you could see that freedom is possible.

By reading these pages, you've witnessed me getting warm and become part of it. When you find your own witness, they can become part of yours.

Our liberation isn't about blindly breaking cultural taboos. The work is about understanding why they exist—to keep our heat trapped—and then breaking them anyway.

Something bigger happens when we let our authentic truth flow back to the places we've abandoned, when we stop fighting this natural flow. We rewrite what's possible for every woman watching.

But you can't do this alone. You need people who can hold your story without trying to fix it, judge it, or make it about them. Safe people who understand that your truth isn't something they need to fix or carry, but is their privilege to witness. These are the people who receive your story with grace instead of judgment, who nod instead of recoil when you share what you've been carrying. When you talk to them, you'll feel the heat starting to flow back to your cold spaces, not because they did anything magical, but because that's what happens when our truth finally has somewhere safe to go.

When you find that person, whether it's a therapist, a trusted friend, or maybe even yourself and a journal at 3:00 a.m., you'll feel it.

Thermal equilibrium is the deepest truth I know about healing. And honestly, it explains why our success has felt so damn impossible, and how to finally make it inevitable.

You Are What's Possible (and You Always Have Been)

My husband has been my steadfast witness for over two decades. While on my morning walk today, we were talking on the phone about this last moment I have with you, this last time we'll be together in this space.

I've avoided sharing so much of what I've written on these pages because I didn't want to be defined by it through anyone else's eyes. Turns out I was already defining it through my own. The purpose of sharing isn't to unload trauma; it's to show you the difference between necessary struggle and unnecessary suffering. Necessary struggle builds us. Unnecessary suffering, what comes from keeping our truth frozen, from treating cultural taboos as sacred instead of recognizing them as devices designed to keep us cold—that's optional.

Kevin reminded me that through it all, at least the parts he's been here to witness, I've always believed that something better was possible. Even when beliefs weighed me down, when circumstances and loss ripped apart my soul. When life felt so uncertain, I held tightly to the belief that I could will myself to be the exception. Deep down was this strong belief that I'd installed when I was just a girl, standing in the doorway, looking at my dad, witnessing this horrible moment. I told myself I'd find my way.

That belief, the utter refusal to accept that this was all there was, is our warmth fighting to flow freely again.

I never thought this book would become another doorway. Not one I stood frozen in, but one I could walk through.

That girl who knew deep down she had stories to tell, even when she couldn't see the path forward. Then me on New Year's Day, deciding to keep a seventeen-year-old promise to myself and finding a way. And then meeting you, hearing your stories, realizing what I needed to do next was going to require all my courage reserves.

Writing this book became my healing. And now I want you to get warm too.

This is what I know about building faith in yourself when the world tells you you don't belong:

The allies and openings you'll need will appear, but only when you stop hiding your truth.

I never planned to become a professional speaker. I didn't even know it was a real job. After my film premiered, I just started saying yes when people asked me to share my story. One invitation led to another, then another. Before I knew it, I was speaking on stages I'd only dreamed of, working with brands I'd admired from afar.

Those early talks were rough. I was trying to fit into this inauthentic corporate version of myself that never worked—trying to sound like other speakers I'd seen, memorizing my keynote word for word, trying to hit certain marks on the stage as I said an impactful line. The breakthrough came when I stopped trying so hard and just showed up as me. Every time I wasn't myself, I paid for it—the point wouldn't land, the joke fell flat. I had to trust myself as I'd never done before.

When I saw the flood of requests and realized how much I loved being onstage, I did what I always do with anything I want to master: I went all in.

I read every book, spoke to anyone who could share insights about the business, and strategically applied to events that felt out of my league, knowing I'd likely be rejected but also that it was just a matter of time before one would say yes. The key was using everything I learned to amplify my authentic voice onstage, not to tone it down. When a major global conference for event planners chose me as their keynote for what felt like a total long shot, it catapulted my career to a whole new level.

None of this happened because I had the perfect credentials or because I waited until I felt ready. It happened because I stopped fighting my thermal equilibrium and let my truth flow.

In my coaching groups over the years, I discovered that we all fall into distinct patterns. The overgiver who disappears into everyone else's needs. The one who never feels qualified enough. The one whose timing never feels quite right. The one who's afraid her success will threaten family relationships. But underneath every pattern was the same thing, just different strategies for keeping our most authentic selves frozen.

Norma proved this to me better than anyone. She was the closest to me in age, and when you're doing this kind of work, peeling back layers, rewriting old rules, something rises up in women our age. Timing. It's easy to wonder whether if it hasn't happened by now, maybe it wasn't meant to be. Maybe the train that would take us to our dream lives has already left the station.

On one particularly memorable call, I asked everyone to identify a single thing they believed was holding them back. Then, they were to create a mantra—the exact opposite of what they were feeling.

Norma blurted out, "My timing is perfect!"

And it stuck. Norma went on to lead the country's largest book club for Latinas; she was featured in Mexican *Vogue* and to this day has publishing giants calling with dream projects.

Norma's breakthrough came from changing her relationship to her timeline, not her circumstances. She stopped keeping her dreams frozen in "someday" and let her heat flow toward "now."

The unexpected allies appeared because she stopped hiding. The opportunities opened because she stopped waiting for everything to line up.

Whenever I feel too late, too old, or like maybe my time has come and gone, I say Norma's mantra.

It's your turn now. Say it with me: *My timing is perfect.*

Because what thermal equilibrium has taught me is that your authentic self has been trying to reach you your entire life. The future you imagined, the voice you stifled, the truth you've kept frozen, they're all still there, waiting for you to stop fighting the flow.

You don't need different credentials. You don't need to be younger (or older), and you don't need anyone's blessing.

You just need to get warm in all the places you've been keeping yourself cold.

The Real Reason

I didn't write this book because I had it all figured out. I wrote it because I was tired of pretending I did. The truth is messy, but it's liberating as hell.

Like the idea that endurance is not strength. That struggle is not a badge. That belonging doesn't come from erasing who we are to make others comfortable.

I wrote it for the woman who's been carrying everyone else while burying herself.

If that's you, I want you to know you don't have to stay frozen to be loved, you don't have to break to begin again. You are not too much and you never were.

Find a witness and tell your story. Even when your voice shakes. Even if you're not sure how this all ends. Tell it anyway. You can trust your story and you can trust that it matters.

Your story is not just yours. It belongs to every woman who's been told to stay quiet, stay small, stay frozen.

Querida, I want you to get warm. In all the spaces that feel cold, make sure to get warm.

So, what will they say?

Let them say . . . she got warm, and we all remembered: We could get warm too.

She roams freely.

Reflection

Okay, amiga, one last thing to try:

Think about your life like that cabin in the woods from Georgie's physics lesson. You have rooms where your authentic heat flows freely, and rooms where you've been working overtime to keep the doors shut.

Make a simple list. On one side write down the areas of your life where you feel most like yourself—where your energy flows naturally. On the other side, write down the areas of your life that feel cold, frozen, and exhausting to maintain. (Hint: You feel stuck, confused, and uncertain when it comes to the things that exist in the cold spaces.)

Maybe it's the promotion you want but won't ask for, the passion project that feels unrealistic or selfish, the family dynamic you pretend is fine, the financial stress you hide.

Here's the thing: I'm not telling you to blow up your life or share every secret tomorrow. But I do want you to notice where you're spending massive amounts of energy fighting your thermal equilibrium.

Pick one small thing from your cold list and take the tiniest action you can:

Schedule that hard conversation about your professional trajectory.

Take one small step toward making that passion project real.

Be honest with yourself about relationships and make a decision accordingly.

Share the price you want to start charging for your services.

Book that solo trip.

Every action, however small, lets warmth back in. Each action restores the energy, until one day you notice you're not fighting the cold anymore—you're finally letting yourself get warm. And you sense the heat was always there. The only thing missing was trusting that you could feel it and still be okay.

ACKNOWLEDGMENTS

To Michelle Herrera Mulligan, my editor, thank you for your unwavering belief in this book and for having my back when I needed it most. Your questions helped me find the balance between love and truth and pulled out the best of this story. I'm so grateful for your mentorship and friendship.

To Norma Perez-Hernandez at Primero Sueño Press, thank you for your loveliness, your ease, and your kindness throughout this entire process.

To Hannah Brattesani, my first agent, thank you for believing in this book from the very beginning. I was so new to this world, and you were nothing but gracious, encouraging, and so patient. You stood by me when we experienced uncertainty and never wavered in your belief that this book would find the right home.

To Marin Takikawa, who stepped into my life with such grace. Thank you for demystifying the industry and guiding me through what was at times a grueling process. You answered every question, never making me feel like an outsider, and cheered me on every step of the way. To the entire team at the Friedrich Agency, thank you for championing this book.

To Esmeralda Santiago, I am profoundly grateful for your guidance. Your generosity was the spark that lit the fuse, and I am honored to walk through the door you helped open.

To Erin Simpson, Emily Varga, and the team at the Simon & Schuster Speakers Bureau, thank you for signing me long before this book existed. Your belief in me and my work has meant the world.

To Richelle Fredson, who helped me find this book's backbone. You took my scattered ideas and shaped them into chapters that made sense. I cannot wait to finally add this one to your stack.

To Suzanne Kingsbury, I'm so grateful to have found you and the Gateless community at the exact perfect time. That final writers' huddle in Cortona, arms wrapped around each other, when you cast a vision for what this book could do and be in the world, gave me the courage to write it with my whole heart.

To Farrah Haidar and Rishma Walji, my writing sisters from Cortona, thank you for reading the earliest chapters of this book and for cheering me on even when I had to step away from our group to write it. Your support has meant everything.

To the wonderful writers I met in Cortona, your stories opened up entire worlds within me and your freedom on the page showed me what was possible with my work.

To Carrie Esposito, for our friendship, our endless voice notes, and for every time you were there to listen, believe, and encourage me. For being willing to read the entire first draft cover to cover, and for that summer weekend trip to the mountains when you told me what you loved, it meant the world.

To Grace Estripeaut, who kept me grounded and focused, never letting me forget why this book matters.

To Theresa Cantley, thank you for the voice notes that felt like lifelines—your consistent check-ins carried me over more humps than you know.

ACKNOWLEDGMENTS

To Eloisa Pérez-Lozano de Castelan, Theresa Gonzalez, and Adriana Rosales, thank you for standing by me all these years. Your belief in me and this work has been unwavering, and I'm so grateful.

To Noni Allwood, who sat in the front row at screening #44 and stayed to offer your belief in me. You wrote "Latinos at Work," one of the most important studies on our community, and you became one of my earliest mentors—opening doors, hosting me in your home, sharing late-night conversations over wine. Thank you for always holding space for the biggest vision of what was possible.

To Jen and Joy, for being ever supportive and curiously present. For all the times you listened for hours about an industry far from your own, celebrating every win with me, and for a friendship that has stood the test of time.

To Amy Torres, Roxanna Damas, and Emma Staniland, women who started as champions of my work within your organizations and, somewhere in between, became dear friends. I'm so grateful to know you.

To my clients, whom I refer to as High Quality Humans, our work together inspired this book. The "line of secrets and dreams" was born at your events, and for that, I'm deeply grateful.

To Rosalia Rivera, Irisneri Alicea Flores, Nancy Flores, and Norma Fabian Newton, thank you for trusting me with your stories and allowing me to share a part of them with the world. Your bravery in reclaiming your voices gave me the permission I needed to finally reclaim mine.

To the women of every cohort of the Eñye Dream Accelerator, Arlyne Solis, Luz Maria Mack, Cynthia Martinez, Theresa Gonzales, Rita Bautista, Nicole Hernandez, Gina Solano, Leslie Puente-Irvin, and all the incredible women who trusted me to guide you for even a small part of your journey. It was a profound honor to travel with you.

To Kevin, my gringo cowboy, thank you for listening, and listening, and listening. For believing in me and reminding me who I was when I doubted. For your tireless encouragement to show the world the "me" that you see every day. Thank you for your steadfastness, for making me feel safe when I'm most afraid, and after all these years, for still making me laugh. I could not have done this without you.

To my daughters, Georgie and Phoebe. Thank you for being patient every time you heard "Mommy is writing," and for understanding when I had to finish "just one last thing" before we could do something fun. For our walk-and-talks, our late-night conversations, and for listening when I read parts of this book to you that I didn't have the words to tell you any other way. You show me every day that these cycles are breakable. You speak up when something doesn't feel right. You ask for what you need. You take up space without apology. Watching you become yourselves is the greatest gift of my life. I adore you, and I respect the young women you are becoming. Being your mom is the favorite chapter of my life. (And, Phoebe, I promise to put you in the sequel, you already know the title.)

To my parents. To my father, whom we lost too soon, I hope I made you proud. And to my mother, thank you for the resilience and the roots. My deep love for my Latinidad begins with you.

To every woman who ever shared a secret with me and who dared to share a dream, our conversations inspired this book. This is for you.

NOTES

Introduction: Why Do Latinas Need This Book?

1. McKinsey & Company and LeanIn.org, *Women in the Workplace 2024: The 10th Anniversary Report,* 2024, 37, https://womenintheworkplace.com/.
2. Noni Allwood and Laura Sherbin, "Latinos Who Repress Their Persona Are More Likely to Rise in the Organization, According to Study," Center for Talent Innovation, September 14, 2016, 1, https://coqual.org/wp-content/uploads/2020/09/LatinosatWork_PressRelease-CTI.pdf.

Chapter Six: Don't Dishonor Your Mother: How to Prioritize Your Own Healing over Fixing Tu Madre

1. Noni Allwood and Center for Talent Innovation, "Latinos at Work: Unleashing the Power of Culture," CTI Report / Coqual, 2016.
2. "A Majority of Latinas Feel Pressure to Support Their Families or to Succeed at Work," Pew Research Center Report, 2024, https://www.pewresearch.org/race-and-ethnicity/2024/05/14/a-majority-of-latinas-feel-pressure-to-support-their-families-or-to-succeed-at-work.
3. Hispanic Star, Hispanic Star Rising (Washington, DC: Hispanic Star, 2026), https://hispanicstar.org/book.
4. Lirio G. Castillo et al., "Construction and Validation of the Marianismo Beliefs Scale," *Psychology of Women Quarterly* 34, no. 1 (March 2010): 121.
5. J. P. Cerdeña et al., "Intergenerational Trauma in Latinxs: A Scoping Review," *Social Science & Medicine* 270 (February 2021): 113662.
6. Luis H. Zayas et al., "Sacrifice for the Sake of the Family: Expressions of Familism by Latina Teens in the Context of Suicide," *Journal of Latinx Psychology* 1, no. 1 (August 2013): 40; and José G. Vargas-Hernández, "The Historical Trauma and Resilience of Individuals of Mexican An-

cestry in the United States: A Scoping Literature Review and Emerging Conceptual Framework," *Social Sciences* 9, no. 5 (May 2020): 83.

7. "Majority of Latinas Feel Pressure," Pew Research Center Report.
8. Alicia Nuñez et al., "A Social Ecological Study of Psychological Distress Among Recently Immigrated, Latina Young Adults," *Journal of Immigrant and Minority Health* 21, no. 4 (August 2019): 748.
9. Ruth C. Cam-Fulbright et al., "The Good Daughter Dilemma: Latinas Managing Family and School Demands," *Journal of Hispanic Higher Education* 12, no. 1 (January 2013): 20–25.
10. Patricia A. Areba-Paez et al., "Familismo, Acculturation, Caregiving Burden with Knowledge of and Confidence in Home Health Services," *Journal of Transcultural Nursing* 29, no. 6 (November 2018): 591.
11. Castillo et al., "Construction and Validation," 122–24.
12. Kenji Yoshino, *Covering: The Hidden Assault on Our Civil Rights* (New York: Random House, 2006), 19–22.
13. LeanIn.org and McKinsey & Company, *Women in the Workplace 2023* (Menlo Park, CA: LeanIn.org, 2023), 10.
14. Sarah Javaid, "Because of the Wage Gap, Latinas Stand to Lose More Than $1.2 Million Over a 40-Year Career," fact sheet (Washington, DC: National Women's Law Center, October 2023).

Chapter Seven: Don't Question the Culture, Part One: Understanding Cultural Inheritance

1. Mark Hugo Lopez, Jens Manuel Krogstad, and Jeffrey S. Passel, "Key Facts About U.S. Latinos," Pew Research Center, September 18, 2023, https://www.pewresearch.org/short-reads/2023/09/18/key-facts-about-us-latinos/.
2. Maria Lopez Twena, "The Duality Framework: Reconstructing the Entravision-Pulpo Research on Latino Consumer Identity," internal research document, Entravision Communications Corporation, 2014–15.
3. "Latinas Are Paid Just 55 Cents for Every Dollar Paid to White, Non-Hispanic Men," fact sheet (Washington, DC: National Women's Law Center, October 2024), https://nwlc.org/resource/latinas-paid-55-cents/.

Chapter Eight: Don't Question the Culture, Part Two: Reinventing Ourselves on Our Own Terms

1. Twena, "The Duality Framework."

ABOUT THE AUTHOR

Denise Soler Cox is an award-winning filmmaker, Top 100 podcaster, and sought-after keynote speaker who transforms how we think about culture, identity, and belonging. After going from stay-at-home mom to internationally recognized belonging expert, she has spoken on over four hundred stages including two TEDx Talks and partnered with world-renowned brands including Ralph Lauren, L'Oréal, Amazon, Microsoft, and JPMorganChase. Her podcast, *The Self-ish Latina,* reached listeners in thirty-two countries and earned Apple Podcasts Featured Host recognition. Cox has appeared as an expert on *NBC Nightly News,* and her work has been featured by *Forbes,* CNN, and PBS.